GOOD
BETTER
BEST
WINES

SECOND EDITION

GOOD
BETTER
BEST
WINES

SECOND EDITION

Carolyn Evans Hammond

ALPHA

Contents

1 **Wine Basics**   **10**

    1 Trade Secrets   12
    2 Getting the Most Out of That Bottle   18

2 **White Wines**   **28**

    3 Chardonnay   30
    4 Pinot Grigio   56
    5 Sauvignon Blanc   70
    6 Other Great Whites   78

3 **Red Wines**   **86**

    7 Red Blends   88
    8 Cabernet Sauvignon   98
    9 Merlot   122
    10 Pinot Noir   130
    11 Other Great Reds   138

4 **Rosé and Sparkling Wines**   **150**

    12 Rosé   152
    13 Sparkling Wine   160

5 | Bargain Wines, Dessert Wines, and Party Wines 172

14	Good Deals at Super-Low Prices	174
15	Dessert Wines	214
16	Party Wines	222

6 | Appendix 240

Hidden Gems	242

Index 248

About the Author 255

Introduction

If anyone can wobble into verbose, irrelevant, wayward, noun-strewn-as-adjective criticism, it's a wine writer. I know. It's my profession. But who cares if the grapes were handpicked by Jean-Paul with the blue beret and his three sons before being thrice sorted, pneumatically pressed, fermented with wild yeasts, aged in large old oak barrels, and blended with 2.4% Sémillon to enhance the mouthfeel? Or that the vines grew in soil rich in calcareous Kimmeridgian clay and Jean-Paul's wife Martine once drank the 1967 vintage with Pierre Bardot, fifth cousin of Brigitte Bardot?

What does the wine taste like? Is it a good price? And is it available at the wine shop or supermarket down the street? That's what matters, especially when you're looking for a great-tasting, five- or ten-buck bottle to enjoy midweek. Sure, a little story is a great conversation starter, but talk of wine can quickly dwindle into mind-parchingly dry drivel about vineyard location, vintage quality, and the tepid tedium of winemaking techniques, such as malolactic fermentation, micro-oxygenation, and filtration.

With this book and the style of wines reviewed in its pages, I'm putting my foot down. Slamming my fist on the table and giving you the stuff that matters. The dirt. The goods. The short, sweet, critical information on what the wine tastes like so you can get on with drinking. I sample, you sip. Deal?

Thus, I've tasted the best-selling brands in the United States. These are brands you know, bottles you recognize, and names you trust to make wines that suit you and everyone you know.

And I'm not pulling these brands from thin air. Each year, a respected market research company called the Beverage Information Group publishes the *Wine Handbook*, which includes a ranking of the top 120 wine brands based on volumes sold across the United States. I've based this book on those brands in the 2017 *Wine Handbook* rankings. Additionally, a few PR people persuaded me to include names outside the top 120 by nearly breaking into arias about the greatness of certain bottles, then anchoring their enthusiasm with compelling information to show that these wines are popular and widely available. So I also tasted these bottles on your behalf.

Just how popular are the brands in this book? The top brand sold the equivalent of 284 million regular-sized bottles in 2016, and most brands represented here sold no fewer than about 5 million bottles in the same 12-month period. These aren't wines people buy, say "meh," and don't buy again. They're repeat purchases. The numbers bear that out. Plus, the wines aren't just stocked at a handful of out-of-the-way wine boutiques; they're the most widely available bottles in the United States. And most of the wines in this book are also available in other major markets.

So what I've done with this guide is compare grapes to grapes. All the $5–$7.99 Chardonnays were tasted side by side to determine which ones are best, as were the $8–$10.99s and the $11–$15 offerings. For this book, $15 is the cutoff because volumes drop considerably beyond that price. Most wines that cost more than $15 are generally made in smaller amounts, aren't as widely stocked, and thus aren't relevant to these pages.

This book also offers a cross-section of the most popular varieties sold in the United States—the Chardonnays, Pinot Grigios, Sauvignon Blancs, Merlots, Cabernet Sauvignons, and so forth—with a chapter devoted to each. To cover some other interesting stuff, a couple catchall chapters called "Other Great Whites" and "Other Great Reds" were added. And to account for the usually terrible but sometimes quite drinkable wine that costs less than $5 per bottle—or the equivalent value in boxed form—I've tacked on a chapter called "Good Deals at Super-Low Prices."

Introduction

I might add that Americans drink more domestic wine than imported, so the regional cross-section of wines here follows suit. A bit of Argentinean, Australian, Chilean, German, Italian, New Zealand, and Spanish wine is included, but there's a whole lot of great-value American stuff.

This book not only recommends the good, better, and best wines in every significant category—with bottle images to help you find them on shelves—but it also slips in other interesting bits of information, including food pairing suggestions, best serving temperatures, and factoids for conversation fodder.

A useful guide to popular wines is necessary given that Americans now drink more wine than any other nation, topping 4.24 billion 750ml bottles in 2016. And the majority of the wines Americans drink are popular big brands that sell for less than $15 per bottle. It makes sense: Although thousands of wines exist, big brands like Bogle, Cavit, Concha y Toro, and Kendall-Jackson deliver great value for the money. They taste pretty much the same year to year, they're widely available, and they sport clear and recognizable labels. And, of course, they're made to appeal to the many rather than the few, so wine drinkers can count on them to not let them down.

While wine snobs with raised pinkies are buying, swirling, and sniffing the wines that cost two arms and a leg per bottle and are tediously hard to find, the rest of Americans are just drinking wine. Popular wine. Big-brand wine. Ironically, a disproportionate amount of wine writing focuses on big-ticket, small-scale wines in infinite detail, but no book had ever focused on ranking popular big brands—until the first edition of this book hit shelves in 2010.

One reason little ink is spilled on big brands is that there's a stigma attached to them. Among wine critics and connoisseurs, they're often seen as less interesting. Too commercial. Too generic. Too industrial—as if quantity has an inverse relationship with quality, which, of course, it doesn't. Uninspiring wines are made by big and small producers, but this stigma persists.

Among some wine critics, it's even believed that big brands are simply a means for driving shareholder value, leading to marketing that overpromises and bottles that underdeliver. Although this is sometimes the case, it's certainly not always true. It makes better business sense to do the opposite: Use economies of scale to make wines that overperform at each price point and then encourage awareness with honest marketing.

Sure, big brands use economies of scale to muscle into the market, and it tugs at the heart to watch cold, hard market forces squeeze out smaller winemakers. With little money to toss toward marketing, merchandising, and advertising and without the quantities of wine or dollars needed to secure wide distribution, the little guy loses and the big guy wins—simple as that. It's especially difficult for wine critics to watch this happen when we spend time visiting smaller winemakers, seeing the dirt under their fingernails, feeling the grip of passion behind their words, and appreciating their daily struggles with those gnarled vines to produce wines of beauty, place, and often pedigree.

On some level, it's hard not to fall in love with these producers when they charm you with their honest lifestyle, take you into their homes, cook you meals, and court you with their most treasured wines lovingly drawn from their cellars. But the people behind the big brands also work hard, and their wines couldn't be successful without consumer consent—without making wine that people like to drink, can find on shelves, and count on for pleasure. Big brands are there to turn to as reliable, go-to wines for Wednesday's pasta, Friday's hamburgers, or that upcoming wedding reception for 100 of your closest friends and family.

The trouble is, with upward of 20 big-brand $8 Chardonnays on the shelf side by side, it's hard to know which one to choose. You certainly can't taste or even smell them all before you buy, and there aren't many scratch-and-sniff labels. So I've taken a good, hard look at—and taste of—the most popular wines in the United States, squirreled out the best in each style and price category, and independently published the results here in this book. For the second time.

Therein lies the purpose of this book. I hope you find it useful.

WINE BASICS

1

Trade Secrets

It's impossible to work in the wine trade and not learn a thing or two that initially surprises you because it runs counter to popular opinion and then seems utterly reasonable when you stop to think about it. Let me give you some examples.

The wine trade teaches you that screw caps aren't just for cheap wines—they work as well as corks for a lot of higher-end wine. You learn that the more expensive wines that critics wax lyrically over comprise a teensy portion of the market. Sure, a disproportionately large amount of ink spilled on the good stuff gives the illusion that everyone's drinking pricey bottles, but that's just not the case. Sometimes, it just means those wines have more budget to hire public relations professionals to send out samples to wine critics, conduct events, and organize press trips.

You also discover that the best big-brand wines are made to taste the same every year, minimizing vintage variation. And that all wine under about $20 is ready to drink upon bottling, so there's no need to worry about aging it. Last but not least, you find makers are starting to put decent wine in boxes these days, so you don't have to steer clear of this category entirely, although it's still prudent to tread carefully. I elaborate on each of these points in this chapter.

A Word on Screw Caps

Which is better: screw cap or cork? I would guess this debate has ruined more dinner parties than you can shake a corkscrew at. And now, with more wine closures used for everyday, popular wines, the potential for more thunderingly boring discussions expands, as typified by the following exchange:

What do you think of screw caps?

Better than plastic stoppers but worse than corks.

You don't say. Why?

Well, screw caps are fine if the winemaker accounts for the wine's technical reaction to that closure during winemaking; otherwise, you end up with dreadful reductive notes....

Reductive?

Dear God. Give me a drink! Is there anything more mentally exhausting than that type of talk? Give me politics, religion, anything—but not wine-bore debates.

To do my small part in preventing tedious discussions on wine closures beyond the confines of wine trade and science circles, I'll end the debate right here. For the kinds of wines we're talking about in these pages, which are bottled young and fresh and meant for immediate consumption, any closure will do. The risk of tasting overbearing flavors of wet cardboard, glue, sulfur, or rotten egg from various wine flaws associated with closures is minimal. They can occur, sure. But the odds are pretty slim. These are among the most popular wines in the United States. If they were frequently badly tainted or terrible, they wouldn't be top sellers—end of story.

If you do find a wine tastes like any of the flavors I noted or is otherwise awful, don't drink it. Open your backup bottle and carry on with your boat cruise, game of strip poker, or evening wind-down drink. Later, take the flawed bottle back to the shop and tell the clerk you think the wine is off. Get a refund and try another bottle.

Most retailers will accept a returned bottle on that basis, but if the merchant is unreasonable, take your business elsewhere. And maybe even Yelp about it.

A Word on Price

Price is a funny thing, and it gets downright comical when you start looking at price categories in the wine trade.

Wines that cost less than $4/750ml are called *value* wine.

Go up a notch to $4–$8 and you're into *popular* wine, which sounds fine until you get to the next two categories: $8–$11 and $11–$15, which are called *premium* and *super premium*, respectively.

Good grief. Where do you go from there?

Well, $15–$20 is considered *ultra premium*, $20–$25 is *luxury*, and anything above that is *super luxury*.

For the purposes of this book, we're sidestepping marketing speak and using dollar signs to symbolize the four relevant per-bottle price brackets, translated into plain English here:

$	Super-low price (under $4.99)
$$	Moderate price ($5–$7.99)
$$$	A little pricier ($8–$10.99)
$$$$	Splurge-worthy price ($11–$15)

Prices do vary from state to state and from store to store, so I've used suggested retail prices to guide the placement of wines in this book. In cases where suggested retail price wasn't included with a wine sample, I categorized bottles based on their average retail price (excluding tax) at www.wine-searcher.com. This website lets you search for a specific wine by name and geographic area and then shows where it's available and at what prices. It's a useful way to comparison shop—but retailers must hate it.

A Word on Vintage and Aging

One of the best things about popular big-brand wines is that they don't vary much from year to year. Like Big Macs, they're made to taste a certain way every time you have them—provided they're stored properly and drunk within a few years of bottling. And to remind you not to worry about dates on bottles, I've omitted vintages entirely from the wines in this book.

Sure, slight quality and flavor variations might occur from year to year, but the whole idea behind big-brand wines is consistency. The winemakers shoot for a signature flavor profile and have a toolbox of methods at hand in the winery to make that happen.

Although big brands taste pretty much the same year after year, always pick the latest vintage on the shelf. It's prudent to do so because all wines under $15 are cast out of the winery ready to drink and are made to be consumed young and fresh.

This brings me to my next point: ageability. Storing a wine to let it improve in the bottle is a bad idea for at least 90% of wines on the market—and pretty much all the wines in this book. If a wine costs under $15, I guarantee it was made for immediate drinking. These wines might stay in their prime for a little while—up to about six years from the vintage date on the bottle for red and up to about three years from that point for white or rosé (and I'm being generous here)—but they won't improve.

Like everything, there are exceptions to the rule. The odd $15 bottle of Cabernet Sauvignon or Syrah might improve with age, but it will still be ready to drink upon bottling. I won't bore you with the technical reasons for this, but wines under $15 aren't meant for aging. Buy them as you need them, keep them reasonably cool, and drink up. (For more on storing wines, see Chapter 2.)

A Word on Packaging

For years, bag-in-box wines were considered horrible—and they typically were. The technology didn't keep the wine fresh for long and the *vin* they put in boxes gave a whole new meaning to the term *vin ordinaire*—the French term for inexpensive table wine.

But technology has improved and better quality wine has been packaged this way. You still have to choose wisely, but now we know bag-in-box wine can give you a perfectly satisfying glass.

The benefits are easy to see: Bag-in-box wines give you a convenient way to drink cheap-and-cheerful wine over the course of days or weeks. They let you keep a variety of wines open at once without worry. And they can stay fresh up to six weeks after opening instead of a couple days or so for a bottle. Plus, they weigh less than glass and obviously don't shatter. The best bag-in-box wines are featured in this book. Here's to Château Cardboard!

2

Getting the Most Out of That Bottle

Did you know that bright light can wreck a bottle of unopened wine within a matter of hours? Absolutely true. And serving a $10 bottle at the right temperature can make it taste like a $20 bottle of wine. Without a doubt, how you store and serve a bottle of wine increases or decreases its pleasure dose dramatically. This chapter reveals secrets to take any wine up a notch and avoid common pitfalls.

Storing It

As noted earlier, all the wines in this book are bottled ready to drink. This means you don't have to worry about correct storage, right? Wrong. You can ruin an unopened bottle quickly by storing it incorrectly. The big wine enemies are: bright light, oxygen, heat, and dramatic temperature fluctuations. I'll explain each in turn.

Bright light

It's a little-known fact that light spoils wine. Bright light from the sun or a lightbulb can make wines smell of onion, cooked cabbage, wet wool, or wet dog—certainly not aromas most of us are looking for in that delicate Pinot Grigio.

A study that looked at the effects of light on wine showed that bottled wines placed about 2 feet from two 40-watt fluorescent lamps in a room at a constant temperature developed off aromas in just 3.3 hours in untinted bottles and 31 hours in tinted bottles.

Getting the Most Out of That Bottle

Most bottles are tinted for this reason, but many aren't. All should be, frankly, to prevent them from acquiring so-called *light-struck* aromas and flavors. Whites and rosés are more susceptible to light damage than reds because tannins inhibit the adverse reactions. And tannins—those naturally occurring compounds in grape skins, seeds, and stems that impart texture to wine—are found in far higher concentrations in reds than whites and rosés.

So it's best to store your bottles in the dark and avoid buying those that appear to have been basking in strong sunlight or close to bright lights at the shop.

Exposure to oxygen

As soon as you open a bottle of wine, it starts to oxidize. This means that after about a day, wine begins to noticeably lose its freshness because of the effects of oxygen. It will start to smell and taste a bit flat and stale instead of fresh and fruity. It will also show less articulate flavors and aromas and taste a little too sharp. Reds oxidize more slowly than whites and rosés, but all wine starts to decline once you open the bottle.

There are a couple ways around this. You can buy canisters of inert gas to squirt into leftover bottles; the gas blankets the wine's surface to block it from oxygen. This method actually works quite well, but you have to keep buying the cans of gas. The other contraption on the market is a fancy pump that vacuums the air out of the bottle to preserve the wine, but I'm not convinced this method works well.

My favorite method for preserving leftover wine is to pour it into a smaller vessel—such as a half bottle—and cork this new container. Assuming the wine reaches the neck of the bottle, it won't be exposed to much oxygen, so you're good for two or three more days. And the best place to store all leftover wine is in the refrigerator to slow down chemical reactions.

Of course, if you're popping that red wine in the fridge, you'll want to take it out about 20 minutes before serving it to let it warm up a tad, as red wine should always be served a bit warmer than straight from the fridge and slightly cooler than room temperature.

Getting the Most Out of That Bottle

Heat

Heat speeds up all chemical reactions, including those that age wine. For a bottle of wine that's at its peak—or "ready to drink," as they say—you don't want to accelerate the aging process or you'll send the wine into a quick decline. Essentially, when a wine declines, the fruit falls out (meaning bright flavors dim and richness diminishes); the alcohol becomes noticeable, felt as heat at the back of the throat; and the whole experience becomes a lot less pleasant. So keep your bottles cool.

Dramatic temperature fluctuation

Storing wine in a place that warms up and then cools down dramatically and repeatedly is another way to force a wine into decline. To prevent this, don't do things like store your bottles near a stove or leave them in the garage when the days are 90°F (32°C) and nights drop to 70°F (21°C). The odd chill won't affect them much, but too many temperature fluctuations are going to ruin your stash.

Serving It

How you serve a wine is as important as its inherent flavor. The fastest way to improve any bottle is by paying attention to the service temperature, glasses, food it's served with, and drinking order.

Temperature

Although it strikes me as a bit obnoxious to use a thermometer to judge the exact temperature of a wine before the pour, it does make sense to pay attention to whether a wine is, say, room temperature, slightly chilled, or ice-cold because you can seriously enhance a wine by serving it at the right temperature.

Color is the first clue. Most of us have heard that reds are best served at room temperature—but that old chestnut has been around for eons, and it no doubt originally referred to the damp chill of a seventeenth-century British country cottage or French château rather than the dry heat of the average centrally heated home in the American suburbs. The big mistake most people make is serving reds too warm, which makes the alcohol stand out rather than the fruit.

Getting the Most Out of That Bottle

A good rule is to put all reds in the fridge for 10–15 minutes before grabbing the corkscrew or twisting the cap. Lighter-bodied reds can chill a little longer than fuller-bodied ones to bring out their inherent refreshment factor.

Whites and rosés are best served a bit cooler than reds. How cold? Depends on the quality of the wine. The better the wine, the less you chill it. Low temperatures hide complexity. So you don't want to overchill better bottles, including but not limited to fine sparkling wines or complex wooded Chardonnays, because you'll lose everything that makes these wines great—and expensive.

On the other hand, if a wine is simplicity itself, has been open a little too long, or is past its best, there's nothing to lose by serving it ice-cold. The extra chill will actually hide shortcomings, such as zero complexity, a bit of oxidation, or a lack of fruit.

Glasses

Does stemware matter? Absolutely. You can double the pleasure of any wine by drinking it from an appropriate glass. It doesn't even have to be expensive really. It just has to be designed so the rim's circumference is smaller than that of the bowl. This feature captures and concentrates a wine's aromas, making a wine seem more intense. And because olfactory glands are far more sensitive than taste buds, this feature is paramount. If you question the importance of your nose in wine appreciation, try tasting something with your nostrils pinched shut.

The other way to use glasses to improve wine is by choosing stemware with the thinnest possible glass or crystal. The thinner the glass, the finer the wine seems. Applying this principal is an effective way to take that vino up a few notches for a special occasion—and save a few dollars.

A huge range of shapes and sizes of wine glasses are now on the market, particularly by high-end companies specializing in designing shapes for every style of wine imaginable. While they do work to enhance the various types of wines, most of us don't have the cupboard space for more than a few wine glass styles. And really, there's no need to go overboard with stemware. A set of larger

Getting the Most Out of That Bottle

glasses for reds, slightly smaller glasses for whites, and some flutes for bubblies should suffice. And if you like, have a set of each in finer glass or crystal for special occasions.

I would even argue that flutes are unnecessary; sparkling wine actually tastes better from white wine glasses because the broader surface area amplifies the all-important aromas. And if you really want to consolidate stemware without compromising quality, a company from Austria called Zalto makes what it calls a "universal" glass, which is handblown and seems to work well with every style of wine—from dry to sweet, red to white, still to sparkling.

Zalto stemware is so thin and lightweight that drinking from it feels like experiential art; they seem barely there, making you feel at one with the wine. They're the thinnest wine glasses I've ever come across—ranging between 0.4 and 0.7 millimeters in thickness.

Zalto isn't cheap. But it might be worth the investment. It's what I own.

Food

There are three basic principles of food and wine pairing, and they might surprise you. While it's usually thought that a wine's color is the most important consideration when matching it to a dish, it's not. A wine's body is actually more significant. A full-bodied white, such as a wooded Californian Chardonnay, can hold up well to heavy dishes, such as risotto, fried pork tenderloin, and even a cheeseboard—all of which are traditionally thought to be best partnered with a red wine.

Meanwhile, a lighter-bodied Pinot Noir or Beaujolais can pair with salmon or poultry just as well as—or sometimes better than—many white wines. And here's a small pearl of wisdom: Body can be determined by a quick glance at the label because it's closely related to alcohol level. Generally, you'll find a light-bodied wine has less than 12% ABV (alcohol by volume), a medium-bodied wine has 12 to 13% ABV, and a full-bodied one exceeds 13% ABV.

The second principle of food and wine pairing is to match the flavor intensity of the dish with that of the wine. It's easy to obliterate the

Getting the Most Out of That Bottle

flavors and aromas of a wine. Obviously, a subtle and restrained Italian Pinot Grigio would be overpowered by grilled sausages, but it would also be overwhelmed by a salad with a too-flavorful dressing. For example, a garlicky Caesar salad would be much better with a richly fruited Chardonnay with a punchy citrus zeal than a gently floral Pinot Grigio. If you think of the flavor intensity rather than just color, you'll find more satisfying selections.

The third big consideration is that a wine should usually be as sweet as or sweeter than the food; otherwise, it can taste unpleasantly thin and acidic. A case in point: dry French Champagne with wedding cake. This pairing ruins the bubbly, which becomes searingly sour with the sugary dessert, and all the marvelous elegance and complexity you're paying for in the wine is lost. Better nuptial couplings would be Champagne with smoked salmon and sweet sparkling wine or even just coffee with the cake.

Some stellar wine-and-dessert matches include Port with chocolate tortes and cakes; Moscato with poached fruit; and Cream Sherry with cheese and figs. For savory-spicy-sweet entrées, such as pad thai, wines with some sweetness work best. Consider the off-dry Riesling, Gewürztraminer, or Moscato. These wines tend to be balanced with crisp, mouthwatering acidity to cleanse and cool the palate.

Drinking order

Wine should always be drunk in the proper order, which is white and rosé before red; light-bodied before full-bodied; dry before sweet; and average before finer quality. And there are solid reasons for this thinking.

Moving from white to red and light-bodied to full lets the palate keep up with the progression. For a dinner party, this might mean serving a crisp sparkling wine as an aperitif, followed by asparagus spears and crab legs with a medium-bodied Sauvignon Blanc, and then ribeye steak and potatoes with a top-notch Californian Cabernet. And sweet wines always follow dry to prevent the latter from seeming too austere. So this menu might end with a succulent, apricot-scented late harvest wine with a fresh fruit tart.

Getting the Most Out of That Bottle

Serving the best quality bottles last guides the palate toward escalating pleasure. If you pour a great wine first, perhaps to showcase it before palates tire, lesser-quality bottles that follow could seem dire.

Tasting It

The business of wine tasting is actually a curious thing. It's different from wine drinking. When I taste a wine wearing my critic's cap, I pull apart the whole pleasure experience. I hold each aspect of the wine up against the cold yardstick of imaginary perfection. Is the fruit concentration and alcohol level in balance or does the alcohol stand out too much? Does the wine taste appealingly crisp or searingly sour? Do the tannins taste velvety and ripe or stalky and green? Is the wine interestingly complex, resonating with five or more identifiable flavors and aromas, or does it seem rather one-dimensional and simple? And how is the typicity?

In other words, does that Pinot Noir taste like a Pinot Noir—or does it taste like it's trying to be a Shiraz? There's no quiet conversation, eye-batting flirtation, suggestive comments, or even jazz. Instead, I'm alone in my home, at a winery, or with other studious wine critics in a lab—spittoon in hand. Yes, I spit; inebriation wreaks havoc on tasting notes.

Bottom line: The whole process is rather clinical. One could argue that tasting this way is too removed from the real drinking experience—and there might be something to that. But there's serious value in technical wine tasting—and it's this: It can determine exactly why a wine does or doesn't taste good and therefore why you probably will or won't like it. Said another way, you might not know why you love or hate a wine, but a wine critic probably would. The technical tasting process yields that insight on a bottle-by-bottle basis.

For example, I guarantee you won't like a wine that's out of balance. If it has too much alcohol for the fruit, it will feel hot in your throat, which isn't what most of us want in our Chardonnay. Or if it lacks a fruit concentration compared with the acidity (a technical term that means sourness), the wine will seem thin and harsh. Bar none,

Getting the Most Out of That Bottle

everybody prefers a wine that's balanced, and wine critics like me assess balance in a cold, calculated, academic way. Curiously, I get some kind of weird pleasure from the whole exercise—and if the banter that ricochets through trade tastings is any indication, other critics share this quirk.

Although all wines in this book have been tasted for technical correctness (because it makes a huge difference as to whether the wine is palatable), I've tried to steer clear of jargon in tasting notes. The point of this little volume isn't to educate you on how to be a wine critic—that's why you've hired me by buying this book; rather, it's to help you drink better wine. Tastier, more satisfying wine. Wine that overdelivers for the price. Wine that thrills.

Although you can't get that deep, gut-hysteria thing going without the right technical composition, the wine style and inherent flavors also have to appeal to you. You probably won't like a Californian Petite Sirah critics wax lyrically over if you like your wines delicate and light. You would have no idea why that restrained, herbaceous Sauvignon Blanc is considered a great value at $15 if you prefer rich, vanilla-scented, oaked Chardonnay.

Do you like tart lime? Drink Riesling. Like creamy vanilla? Drink oaked Chardonnay. Like black currant? Drink Cabernet Sauvignon. Like raspberries? Drink Pinot Noir.

To help, I've explained exactly what each grape varietal tastes like in the first sentence or two of the relevant chapter. You can take it from there because if there's one truism to wine appreciation, it's this: Tasting for pleasure is a personal thing.

PART **2**

WHITE WINES

BERINGER
FOUNDERS' ESTATE®

CHARDONNAY
CALIFORNIA

Brothers Jacob & Frederick founded Beringer
in 1876, believing Napa could produce
world-renowned wines.

The longest continually
operating winery in California.

OUR FOUNDERS

3

Chardonnay

In its pure form, Chardonnay (pronounced *shar-don-NAY*) is crisp and refreshing, with flavors and aromas reminiscent of apple, citrus, and tropical fruit. When aged or fermented in oak, the fruit becomes imbued with a warm creaminess that calls to mind vanilla, buttered toast, nuts, caramel, or warm spice notes.

It's fashionable these days to say you hate Chardonnay, but it's the most popular wine in the United States and has been for the last decade, with sales increasing every year. In fact, about one-fifth of all wine sold in the United States is Chardonnay. It remains one of the most planted, produced, and sought-after varietals in the world and is made in almost every wine region on the planet.

Chardonnay is fascinating in its variability. Stylistically, it swings from the lean, linear austerity of fine French Chablis and other cool climate, unwooded styles to ripe, creamy expressions from warmer climates, such as California and Australia, imbued with an unmistakable stroke of oak. And between those extremes, every shade of Chardonnay imaginable exists.

In truth, it would be difficult to hate all types of Chardonnay. This chapter is chock-full of some gorgeous versions.

$$ Chardonnay

Woodbridge
CALIFORNIA

Quiet aromas of mixed citrus
and sliced apple lead to a
bright, clean attack of the same
edged with toasted oak.
Although this wine is a bit
simple and lacks the
concentration and complexity
of some of its competitors, it's
balance offers fair value for the
money. Medium-bodied with
13.5% ABV.

Lindeman's Bin 65
AUSTRALIA

This popular wooded
Chardonnay tastes rich and full-
fruited, with a generous and
juicy pineapple–citrus core
imbued with creamy notes of
toasted nut. Great weight and
fruit saturation buoyed by
balancing acidity—a total
sunshine-in-the-glass style.
Good value. Medium- to full-
bodied with 13.5% ABV.

BEST

Flipflop
CALIFORNIA

Fresh and tart tasting, this zippy little Chardonnay scrapes the palate clean with its unbridled blast of key lime and ripe pineapple. It's a racy refresher that tastes lit from within and lingers for ages on the palate. There's a hint of sweetness, but it's hidden beneath the wild gust of mouthwatering acidity. Frivolous but enchanting. Medium-bodied with 13% ABV.

Did You Know?
A bottle of Lindeman's Bin 65 Chardonnay is consumed 80 million times per year in more than 100 countries.

Food Pairing Tip
I like to pair big, wooded Chardonnays with richer foods, such as fried fish, pasta in a cream sauce, or even salted potato chips. Doing so brings the bright citric character to the forefront and transforms the wine into a more delicate-tasting drop while maintaining enough weight and power to hold its own.

Ideal Serving Temperature
Simple, crisp, unoaked Chardonnays should be served cold—perhaps straight from the fridge—while complex, creamy, oaked versions are best a few degrees warmer. Low temperatures hide subtle flavors and aromas, so let your nose and palate guide you when judging the best temperature for serving.

$$ Chardonnay

**Beringer
Main & Vine**
CALIFORNIA

While this Chardonnay hints at lemon and green apple on the nose and palate, there's really not much else going on. It's clean and well made, yes; but if you're buying Beringer, trade up because that's where the real value for the money begins. Medium-bodied with 13% ABV.

**Sutter Home
Family Vineyards**
CALIFORNIA

Although this wine shows little aroma, the reservedness vanishes on the palate with a juicy onslaught of tropical and citrus fruits. While not particularly articulate in its flavor definition, its ripe, dry, satiny, crisp character is a pleasure to drink. Medium-bodied with 13% ABV.

BEST

Fish Eye
SOUTH EASTERN
AUSTRALIA

Tasting a bit like a great summer vacation in a glass, this sprightly little white wine just takes you away from it all. Expect a riveting wash of perfectly ripe melon, crisp red apple, and pear that gives way to a creamy vanilla finish that lingers. Tastes dry but not bone-dry—just impeccably balanced. Medium-bodied with 13.5% ABV.

Behind Fish Eye Wines
According to Australian lore, a fisherman with an especially good catch is said to have the "fish eye"—a sixth sense about what will attract a fish's attention. Does Fish Eye Winery have a sixth sense about what will attract the attention of wine lovers? It certainly seems so with this Chardonnay.

Beware!
Some Chardonnays can rise to 15% ABV—and that's a lot. If it's that level or more, it often tastes too hot in the throat, making it unpleasant and unbalanced. One of the best ways to cut the risk of dissatisfaction is to check the ABV before you buy.

Did You Know?
Beringer has made more *Wine Spectator* Top 100 appearances than any other winery in history. Beringer Vineyards is the oldest continuously operating winery in Napa Valley because it sold sacramental wine during prohibition.

$$ Chardonnay

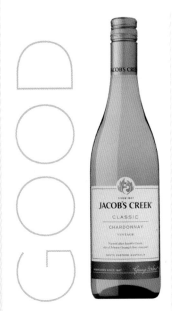

Jacob's Creek Classic
AUSTRALIA

Clean and balanced, this is a decidedly average-tasting Chardonnay. It's got the usual citrus and apple flavors of Chardonnay; a bit of glinting acidity to keep it tasting fresh; and some vanilla notes that reveal a bit of oak treatment. But it lacks the finesse to make it "better" or "best" among its competitors in this book. Medium-bodied with 12.8% ABV.

Canyon Road
CALIFORNIA

Love the pretty perfume of honeysuckle and white peach this wine gently exudes before racing across the palate all crisp and clean. Lively flavors call to mind a perfect peach pie. Juicy-tart stone fruit, toasty butter pastry, and a sprinkle of nutmeg and cinnamon—it's all here in spades. Medium-bodied with 13% ABV.

BEST

> ### Counting Calories?
> Almost all wines contain sugar and alcohol, which is where the calories are, but the vast majority of the calories come from the alcohol, not the sugar. This is because alcohol is dense in calories. A single gram of alcohol packs seven calories, which is almost double that of sugar (four calories per gram), and most wines contain far more alcohol than sugar. If you want to cut calories, keep an eye on the ABV number and try to drink wines with 12.5% ABV or less.

Sycamore Lane
CALIFORNIA

Gentle aromas of white blossoms and lemon zest lead to a bracing attack of orange oil that flirts with lemon sorbet and toasted coconut. This wine is instantly captivating, then tapers slowly to a finish of tropical fruits and nuts. Delightful little wine for the money. Medium-bodied with 13% ABV.

$$ Chardonnay

[yellow tail]
SOUTH EASTERN
AUSTRALIA

Although clean and balanced, the flavors and aromas of this wine are indecipherable. They sort of give the impression of stewed peach and cooked apple with some lemon-squirt acidity, but there's not much stylishness going on in terms of well-cut flavors. Overall, it's just a basic Chardonnay. Medium-bodied with 13% ABV.

Barefoot
CALIFORNIA

Aromatic and engaging scents of mixed citrus lead to round, restrained flavors of Gala apple, honeydew, ripe apricot, and a light, velvety touch of vanilla. This wine feels pillowy soft in the mouth, with a kiss of sweetness. Chill it well to amp up the zip. Medium-bodied with 13.5% ABV.

Did You Know?

Mezzacorona is the largest producer of Chardonnay in Italy and consistently produces one of the top-selling Italian Chardonnays in the United States.

Mezzacorona
Estate Bottled
DOLOMITI, ITALY

This cool, crisp, gently oaked wine suggests apple butter slathered on oven-warm bread, with hints of toasty oak. It's a bit more restrained than most New World renditions of this grape variety, imparting a certain delicacy and elegance that's rather fetching. Fabulous food wine because it won't upstage or clash with anything on the plate. Medium-bodied with 13% ABV.

$$$ Chardonnay

Gnarly Head
CALIFORNIA

While clean and correct, this wine doesn't offer the concentration of its direct competitors. The flavors are wispy and light, suggesting cool melon and Golden Delicious apple, with a shock of brisk citric zeal and a short finish. Mediocre. Medium-bodied with 13.5% ABV.

Cupcake
MONTEREY COUNTY, CALIFORNIA

Not surprisingly, this Chardonnay calls to mind vanilla layer cake—a nicely browned sponge, vanilla buttercream, and a rich and creamy mouthfeel. The opulence is reined in by taut acidity, and unlike the name might suggest, the wine is bone-dry. Overall, a well-made and generous wine for the money. No wonder it's wildly popular! Medium-bodied with 13.5% ABV.

Food Pairing Tip

Great matches for gently oaked Chardonnay include grilled salmon, chicken in cream sauce, and a cheese board of Gruyere, Havarti, and Camembert. It also tastes stellar with a Caesar salad, gourmet macaroni and cheese, or broiled lobster tails with drawn butter.

Beringer
Founders' Estate
CALIFORNIA

Light, pretty scents of lemon zest and poached pear lead to an upsurge of full-throttle fruit that unfurls with flavors of sweet, juicy pear and bright green apple edged gently with warm wood. The raging eruption of flavor tastes energetic and sunlit, driving through to a strong finish. Sumptuous wine with a sense of cohesion and purpose. Full-bodied with 13.9% ABV.

$$$ Chardonnay

Smoking Loon
The Original
CALIFORNIA

From the gentle note of orange oil on the nose to the swell of mixed citrus, peach jam, and honeyed lemon edged with toasty oak, this ripe little number offers good value. Definitely a clean, creamy–fresh expression of wooded Chardonnay. Medium- to full-bodied with 13.5% ABV.

Sterling Vineyards
CALIFORNIA

Pure, balanced, and judiciously oaked, this Chardonnay is a standout buy. Scents of apricot, pear, and baked goods lead to a fresh burst of cool, lively fruit. Think glossy flavors of baked and buttered apple, wet stones, and apricot Danish pastry doused with a tight seam of acidity that reins in the fruit. Well balanced and well made. Medium-bodied with 13.5% ABV.

Chardonnay **$$$**

Did You Know?
Sterling Vineyards is the #1 most visited winery in Napa Valley, hosting more than 200,000 guests each year. The winery is perched atop a hill with broad views of the valley.

Wine and Music Connections
Upbeat pop tunes can make Chardonnay taste more "zingy and refreshing," according to findings from researchers at Heriot-Watt University in Edinburgh. The results were attributed to "cognitive priming theory," meaning music sets up the brain to respond to wine in a certain way.

Bogle Vineyards
CALIFORNIA

Enticing aromas of crème brûlée draw you toward the ripe, crisp, full-on attack of juicy pear, cooked apple, and cream. Hints of vanilla, caramel, oak, and nutmeg add interest to this complex, concentrated thriller with considerable length. This wine might just become your new favorite crush. Medium- to full-bodied with 13.5% ABV.

$$$ Chardonnay

Noble Vines Collection 446
CALIFORNIA

Here's a hefty style of wooded Chardonnay heaving with flavors of poached pear and cantaloupe, with a creamy–crisp center and powerful notes of coconut, toasted almonds, and vanilla custard. A long hot-buttered popcorn taste lingers on the finish. Good value. Full-bodied with 14.5% ABV.

Fetzer Sundial
CALIFORNIA

Scents of honeydew lead satiny flavors of mango, pineapple, melon, and warm figs. Such a beautifully ripe, focused, pure-tasting wine with a well-balanced structure and a long buttery finish. Total crowd-pleaser. Medium-bodied with 13.5% ABV.

BEST

For the Love of Mother Earth

Fetzer Vineyards was the first winery in California to operate solely on renewable energy in the form of solar power and the first winery to be officially zero waste.

Did You Know?

Chardonnay is an ancient grape variety thought to have originated in Lebanon—not France, which is widely considered the grape's heartland today.

Toasted Head Barrel Aged
CALIFORNIA

If you like caramel apples, you'll love this wine. It tastes like perfectly ripe apples layered with buttery caramel. The precision of these two complementary flavors, the silky–smooth texture, and long finish create a hedonistically appealing wine. Full-bodied with 14.5% ABV.

$$$ Chardonnay

Dark Horse
The Original
CALIFORNIA

Aromas of ripe melon lead to a soft, round surge of fresh fig, mango, and melon with a sprinkle of nutmeg on the finish. Because this is a mellow, easygoing style of Chardonnay that's more buttery than crisp, chill it well to amp up the refreshment. Medium-bodied with 13.5% ABV.

Smoking Loon
Steelbird
CALIFORNIA

Expect crisp apple flavors spiked with cool steel and salt notes. The effect is a well-cut, lean, and linear style of unoaked Chardonnay, with just enough flesh to add focus and balance. Delicious value. Medium-bodied with 13.5% ABV.

Columbia Crest Grand Estates
COLUMBIA VALLEY, WASHINGTON

Classic wooded Chardonnay with lashings of glossy, buttery, caramelized fruit—mostly apples but also peaches. The fleshy layers are also threaded with warm baking spices—cinnamon, nutmeg, and allspice—as well as a light topcoat of vanilla. This is a gorgeous, intelligent-tasting, oaked Chardonnay. Medium- to full-bodied with 13.5% ABV.

Burgundy's Chardonnay

Although it's generally agreed among wine experts that Burgundy makes some of the finest Chardonnay in the world, you won't often find the grape variety printed on the labels. Instead, you'll find the region, district, commune, or vineyard names on Burgundian labels. The premise is that place of origin matters more than grape variety because a wine is a product of its "terroir"— the compilation of geographic place, climate, weather, grape, and soil.

$$$$ Chardonnay

Bonterra
MENDOCINO COUNTY,
CALIFORNIA

This wine rushes in with an almost aggressive mix of tropical fruit, fresh citrus, and white flowers, followed by a light undertow of toasted almond. Although the flavors are well toned and expressive, the wine lacks the polish and seamlessness of its direct competitors. Medium-bodied with 13.3% ABV.

Estancia Vineyards
MONTEREY COUNTY,
CALIFORNIA

Lush, heady aromas of honeyed peaches and tart pineapple lead to the same flavors amplified on the palate. Then, after the initial flush of fruit fades, underpinnings of hazelnut, vanilla bean, coffee, and dark maple syrup emerge and resonate. Medium-bodied with 13.5% ABV.

Chardonnay $$$$

Hey, It's Organic!
Bonterra Chardonnay is made from 100% organically grown grapes. Bonterra wines have been organic since the winery's inception in 1987.

Did You Know?
Chardonnay remains California's most widely planted wine grape, with 94,532 acres of it reported in 2016. Also that year, California crushed 676,000 tons of Chardonnay.

BEST

Chateau St. Jean
SONOMA COUNTY, CALIFORNIA

Invigorating aromas of tangerine and citrus confit smell glossy and cool. Then, on the palate, restrained flavors of the same create a smooth attack infused with buttered toast, marzipan, grapefruit pith, and orange blossom. Such complexity and precision! A stylish, grown-up tasting wine with a fine cushion of creaminess. Medium-bodied with 13.6% ABV.

$$$$ Chardonnay

Josh Cellars
CALIFORNIA

Oodles of fresh oranges and lemons flood the senses on the nose and palate before a quiet undertow of hazelnut elongates the finish. Then a final twist of lemon oil leaves the palate perfectly cleansed and seasoned. Lovely juice. Medium-bodied with 13.5% ABV.

Alamos
MENDOZA, ARGENTINA

This rich, citrus-laden expression is layered with a mélange of white peach purée and sun-soaked apricot lightly laced with honeysuckle, vanilla, and chalk. Compelling, sassy, and nuanced Chardonnay with deft oak integration. Medium-bodied with 13% ABV.

Food Pairing Tip

Don't hesitate to pair a full-bodied wooded Chardonnay with meat—even grilled steak. The weight of the wine will usually stand up well to beefy flavors, while the tight seam of acidity will refresh the palate beautifully between bites.

BEST

Columbia Winery
COLUMBIA VALLEY, WASHINGTON

A light, sprightly lift of cool lemon draws you toward a polished wash of lemon curd flavor. A moment later, it rises, arcs, and unfurls with creamy mango, oyster shell, American oak, lime zest, and salt that lingers for ages. This is a serious and complex-tasting wine at a remarkably low price. Full-bodied with 13.8% ABV.

$$$$ Chardonnay

Chateau Souverain
CALIFORNIA

Expect a swift hit of bright lemon and green apple that tastes tart and offers instant refreshment but soon reveals a certain hollowness mid-palate. The underlying oak influence soon comes to the forefront and lingers in the background. It's a clean, crisp Chardonnay that could use a little more complexity and concentration to make it interesting. Full-bodied with 13.9% ABV.

Kendall-Jackson Vintner's Reserve
CALIFORNIA

This stately white exudes evocative aromas of toasted nut, vanilla cream, and pithy citrus peel before slipping silky swift across the palate. Mouthcoating flavors of crisp apple woven with warm hazelnut, crème brûlée, and buttered toast taste dignified and shiny—not overdone. Medium-bodied with 13.5% ABV.

BEST

Edna Valley Vineyard
CENTRAL COAST, CALIFORNIA

Bags of orchard fruit—all freshly picked and sliced—saturate the palate before fading to reveal a ripple of cinnamon, nuts, praline, and white pepper. This well-toned Chardonnay caresses the palate with its satiny texture, while tense acidity keeps it vigorous and poised. Distinguished tasting. Full-bodied with 14.9% ABV.

$$$$ Chardonnay

Chateau Ste. Michelle
COLUMBIA VALLEY,
WASHINGTON

White pepper and lemon oil
aromas lead to a zesty palate of
grapefruit pulp and mixed citrus
oil layered with a discreet dash
of baking spices, especially
allspice and clove. It's firmly
sculpted but not quite as
smooth tasting as many of its
competitors. Medium-bodied
with 13.5% ABV.

Oyster Bay
MARLBOROUGH,
NEW ZEALAND

This wine is a fine example of
Marlborough's full-throttle
Chardonnay. Wildly exuberant,
it douses the palate with
energetic flavors of Granny
Smith apples and key lime—all
uncluttered and ample. Then
the high-voltage fruit slowly
gives way to a touch of creamy
nougat that lingers on the finish.
Well made. Medium-bodied
with 13.5% ABV.

Historic Winery

In 1936, Wente was the first winery in California to produce a varietal-labeled Chardonnay—made from its heritage Wente clones. Now nearly 80% of the Chardonnay vineyards in California are planted with the Wente clone, which originated from the Wente family estates.

Did You Know?

Oyster Bay Marlborough Chardonnay is the best-selling New Zealand Chardonnay in the United States by volume.

Wente Morning Fog
CALIFORNIA

This toasty, barrel-aged Chardonnay tastes refined and harmonious as it swathes the palate with creamy–crisp flavors of best-ever lemon meringue pie, followed by a resonant finish of toasted coconut and vanilla. Here's a wine that's quietly assertive, graceful, and full of charm. Medium-bodied with 13.5% ABV.

RUFFINO

◆ DAL 1877 ◆

LUMINA

PINOT GRIGIO

DELLE VENEZIE

Indicazione Geografica Tipica

4

Pinot Grigio

Pinot Grigio (pronounced *pee-no GREE-gee-oh*) is a petal-light wine with feathery strokes of lemon-lime and floral notes.

Despite the fact wine snobs scorn Pinot Grigio for being too neutral, too bland, and much too characterless to be taken seriously, Americans love Pinot Grigio. In the last 15 years or so, its popularity has skyrocketed. And why not? While much of it might be neutral, some of it is simply clean, elegant, honest refreshment. And the best Pinot Grigio possesses a gentle floral–stony character rather than simply featureless fruit.

But Pinot Grigio isn't new. Italians have been drinking it for years all over the old boot. They tend to drink it with fish from waters off the eastern seaboard because it's a perfect pairing. Pinot Grigio's understated nature doesn't upstage seafood with strong flavors and aromas—it just enhances it.

While some of the finest Pinot Grigio still comes from Italy, New World producers from California and Australia are also making some outstanding versions—as you'll discover in this chapter.

$$ Pinot Grigio

Lindeman's Bin 85
SOUTH EASTERN AUSTRALIA

Lime leaf and nougat aromas lead to a quick hit of raw acidity that obliterates any nuance that might have otherwise been apparent. Racy and a bit inelegant with little fruit character other than the allusion of lemon and lime. Light-bodied with 12% ABV.

Bella Sera
VENETO, ITALY

Gentle aromas of honeysuckle and pear lead to a vibrant hit of salted lemon zest and sliced lime with a certain wet stone center underneath. Undeniably charming, this focused wine tastes elegant, pure, and saline—dignified even. Light-bodied with 12% ABV.

It's a Fact
Pinot Grigio grapes range from bluish-gray to brownish-pink, traditionally producing a rusty-colored or slightly pinkish wine. In 1961, Santa Margherita became the first winery to use the grapes to make a pure white wine. They did this by limiting the grape skins' contact with the juice to avoid acquiring color—a technique perfected by the French in Champagne. Now most Pinot Grigios are quite pale white wines.

Placido
TUSCANY, ITALY

An instant whiff of flint and chalk rise from the glass before the brisk attack races across the palate, cascading with flavors of sour lemon, wet stones, and salt. The stony–salty, slightly savory character persists on the finish for ages. Although the style might be a bit austere for some, this is quite a stylish, understated little wine with lots going on. Amazing value. Light-bodied with 12.5% ABV.

$$ Pinot Grigio

WHITE WINES

Black Box
CALIFORNIA

Not one of the better or best wines, to be sure, this Pinot Grigio tastes thin and slightly lacking in the tight, bright crispness one looks for with this variety. Expect nondescript flavors hinting vaguely toward mixed citrus. There are better choices at this price. Light-bodied with 12.5% ABV.

Flipflop
CALIFORNIA

Casual but polished, this focused, fresh, and fruit-forward style of Pinot Grigio tastes like the best gourmet lemon-lime sorbet you've ever tasted—in adult form. The kiss of sweetness offsets the taut, mouthwatering acidity to create impeccable balance, while the saturated center tastes sunlit and pure. Light- to medium-bodied with 13% ABV.

BEST

Folonari
VENETO, ITALY

Delicate aromas of lime leaf and chalk lead to polished, silky flavors of the same imbued with breezy hints of wildflowers, lemon zest, and minerals, with a touch of white pepper and chalk on the finish. This wine is delicate and supple while remaining vibrant and focused. Solid buy. Light-bodied with 11.5% ABV.

$$ Pinot Grigio

Rex Goliath
The Giant 47 Pound
Rooster
AUSTRALIA

Apparently, this wine is a tribute to the larger-than-life personality of a 47-pound rooster that lived at the turn of the twentieth century. Expect an immediate and mouth-filling swirl of tart lime sorbet laced with feathery floral notes. So much exuberance that it tastes a bit flamboyant. Light-bodied with 12% ABV.

Fish Eye
SOUTH EASTERN
AUSTRALIA

Gentle scents of lemon oil lead to an arresting wash of bright lemon, tangerine, and pink grapefruit. While not the most refined or restrained style of Pinot Grigio on the shelf, it's pure tasting, with heaps of clean, vibrant, well-defined fruit shot through with electric acidity. Surefire and full-fruited refreshment. Light-bodied with 12.5% ABV.

Barefoot Pinot Grigio Sour Recipe

Make this delicious drink featuring Pinot Grigio.

Ingredients
2oz Barefoot Pinot Grigio
1oz orange juice
½oz lemon juice
½oz simple syrup

Directions
1. In a cocktail shaker, combine Pinot Grigio, orange juice, lemon juice, simple syrup, and ice. Shake to blend and chill.
2. Strain into a glass over fresh ice. Garnish with orange slices and whole cherries.

Barefoot
CALIFORNIA

Soft aromas of tangerine lead to a lick of the same layered with yellow plum and a hint of slate somewhere. Love the sleek texture, impeccable balance, and sure-footed restraint—all of which comes together to put this wine ahead of the competition. Light-bodied with 12% ABV.

$$$ Pinot Grigio

Stemmari
SICILY, ITALY

From the southernmost part of Italy, this ripe, round expression of Pinot Grigio is chockful of ripe ruby grapefruit oil and peach flavor. But it lacks the racy acidity most look for in this style of wine. There's some tension and an attractive dusting of salt on the finish that leaves the palate squeaky clean, but better bottles line shelves at this price. Light-bodied with 12.5% ABV.

Cavit Collection
VENETO, ITALY

This classically styled Italian white zips across the palate with poise and grace, upheld by a tightly wound core of gentle lemon and Granny Smith apple. It's crisp and refreshing with a glossy mouthfeel and resonant finish. Solid value. Light-bodied with 12% ABV.

It's a Fact

Cavit Collection is the best-selling Pinot Grigio in North America.

Food Pairing Tip

Pinot Grigio is easy-to-sip and gastronomically versatile. It goes particularly well with simply prepared seafood and poultry, but it's also terrific with spice noodle dishes.

Dark Horse
The Original
CALIFORNIA

Languid aromas of chalk and salted lemons lead to a crisp hit of the same layered with gentle floral notes, cool marble, and a quiet saline finish. This is quite a dignified expression of Pinot Grigio, with a lean, well-toned structure and classy restraint. Medium-bodied with 13.4% ABV.

$$$ Pinot Grigio

The Original Smoking Loon
CALIFORNIA

Flavors and aromas of mandarin zest and lemon curd taste opulent and robust before slowly tapering to an invigoratingly crisp lime finish. This isn't an understated Pinot Grigio, to be sure, although the taut seam of acidity reins in the flourish of flashy fruit. Not terribly complex but refreshing and pure. Light-bodied with 12.5% ABV.

Mezzacorona Estate Bottled
TRENTINO, ITALY

This glossy, pale, straw-colored wine shows only the lightest strokes of lemon on the nose before sliding across the palate with sleek flavors of creamy lime sherbet, and a puff of smoke somewhere. Fresh and nervy style with dry minerals on the finish that taste like struck flint. Easy crowd-pleaser. Light-bodied with 12.5% ABV.

Drink Up!
Because Pinot Grigio is always meant to be drunk young and fresh, grab the latest vintage available on the shelf.

**Ruffino
Lumina**
VENETO, ITALY

Pretty lime blossom and talc scents rise from the glass. Then seductive flavors quietly suggest tangy lemon curd edged with crushed stones and raw almonds. The flavors taste beautifully harmonious and taper to a long salted lemon finish. This is a relatively sophisticated-tasting Pinot Grigio for the money. Light-bodied with 12% ABV.

$$$$ Pinot Grigio

Estancia Vineyards
CALIFORNIA

Although well balanced and crisp, this bottle is quite atypical for a Pinot Grigio. It lacks the light body and delicacy most look for in this wine style. Expect a quick blast of tangerine, passion fruit, and mango on the nose and palate—and not much elegance. Medium- to full-bodied with 13.5% ABV.

Mezzacorona Cliffhanger Vineyards
TRENTINO, ITALY

Quiet aromas that suggest white grapefruit and golden pear waft gently from the glass. Then delicate flavors of grapefruit oil, nougat, and raw nut roll in. Although this is stylistically a restrained and fine-boned wine, it could still use a bit more concentration to score a "best" ranking here. Light- to medium-bodied with 13% ABV.

Pinot Grigio $$$$

Food Pairing Tip

Ecco Domani Pinot Grigio tastes fabulous when paired with pesto, spinach, and mozzarella grilled cheese; Asian teriyaki; and roasted pumpkin seeds.

BEST

Ecco Domani
VENETO, ITALY

Seductive dry-roasted cashew and Brazil nut aromas give way to a swift hit of tightly stitched lemon and pineapple. Then resonant allusions of raw almond and hazelnut return on the finish. With seamless texture, bone-dry appeal, and bracing acidity, this wine offers outstanding value. Medium-bodied with 12.5% ABV.

Oyster Bay wines capture the
special character of New Zealand
— elegant, assertive wines with
glorious fruit flavours

MARLBOROUGH

Sauvignon Blanc

Oyster Bay

NEW ZEALAND

5

Sauvignon Blanc

Sauvignon Blanc (pronounced *sew-vin-yown BLONK*) refreshes like a thing possessed. Mouthwatering green strokes of flavor attack the palate like no other, recalling damp herbs, asparagus, cut grass, lime, and gooseberry.

These wines complement salads, pestos, fish dishes, and herbed chicken beautifully; they don't generally cost a fortune; and they taste like pure magic served with asparagus spears drizzled with good olive oil and sprinkled with sea salt. Although the wine's natural lime-squirt acidity refreshes the palate between mouthfuls of all sorts of oily or buttery dishes, making it a great food wine, the gooseberry-drenched versions from Marlborough, New Zealand, make brilliant cocktail-style wines to sip on their own or with salty finger foods. Classic Marlborough Sauvignon Blanc with its full-throttle fruit bumps almost all other wines to take top place for quintessential quencher.

In short, the best Sauvignon Blancs are wonderfully balanced spheres of flavor that roll around on your tongue and tickle your fancy in the most titillating way. To see what I mean, try a few bottles recommended in this chapter.

$$ Sauvignon Blanc

Woodbridge
CALIFORNIA

A soft perfume of lime blossoms leads to a tangy attack of lime purée and grapefruit edged with damp herbs and salt. Bone-dry and tasty but just a little rough around the edges—not quite as seamless as its competitors. Light-bodied with 12% ABV.

[yellow tail]
93% AUSTRALIA
7% NEW ZEALAND

Asparagus and gooseberry aromas leap out of the glass before a racy attack of damp herbs, lime, and gooseberries follow. The mid-palate tastes slightly hollow, meaning it could use a little more concentration, but overall, it's not a bad little Sauvignon Blanc for the money. Certainly well balanced, clean, and approachable. Light-bodied with 12% ABV.

Did You Know?
Sauvignon Blanc originates from Bordeaux in France.

What's in a Name?
Sauvignon Blanc comes from the French words "sauvage," which means wild, and "blanc," which means white. It's thought to have this name because its a French indigenous grape variety.

Barefoot
CALIFORNIA

Poached pear and candied lime aromas draw you toward a crisp entry that's surprisingly bone-dry and brimming with lime zest and green pear flavors laced with a whisper of fresh rosemary. A long, salted lime oil finish completes the experience. Quite a refined little wine for a wine called "Barefoot." Light- to medium-bodied with 13% ABV.

$$$ Sauvignon Blanc

Cupcake
MARLBOROUGH,
NEW ZEALAND

This wine is all about pure, unadulterated refreshment with its shock of electric acidity. A tightly wound core of Meyer lemon, passion fruit, and gooseberries tastes focused and fresh, with a persistent finish. Light-bodied with 12.5% ABV.

Nobilo
MARLBOROUGH,
NEW ZEALAND

Classical Marlborough here. Aromas of gooseberry, lemongrass, and elderflower rise from the glass before the brisk yet somewhat delicate attack of lime purée, gooseberry, grapefruit, and lemongrass follow. Fresh, crisp, and dry. Medium-bodied with 13% ABV.

Food Pairing Tip

You can enjoy absolutely any Sauvignon Blanc with a bucket of fried chicken and the pairing will sing.

Concha y Toro Casillero del Diablo
CHILE

Understated scents of crisp green apple lead to a satiny-smooth, salivatingly fresh expression with much charm. Well-integrated flavors of green apple, wild herbs, lime oil, and sea spray unravel slowly and resonate on the finish. Outstanding effort by this reputable Chilean maker. Medium-bodied with 13% ABV.

$$$$ Sauvignon Blanc

Joel Gott
CALIFORNIA

This is a gutsy Sauvignon Blanc with a firm, muscular core and bold flavors of sun-drenched grapefruit, lime purée, and saturated tropical fruit. Forward and hefty for a Sauvignon Blanc. Full-bodied with 13.9% ABV.

Josh Cellars
NORTH COAST, CALIFORNIA

Faint aromas of lemons and white flowers lead to a zippy attack of pineapple and lemon-lime sorbet. A bright and lively little wine with dynamic energy, a lustrous mouthfeel, and a delicately tapered finish that ends with a final note of chalk. Medium-bodied with 13% ABV.

Food Pairing Tip

Oyster Bay Sauvignon Blanc pairs fabulously with pan-fried fresh fish or scallops, spinach- and ricotta-stuffed cannelloni, pad thai, or oven-roasted asparagus with shaved Parmesan.

Oyster Bay
MARLBOROUGH,
NEW ZEALAND

With wafting aromas of homemade lime marmalade on freshly baked bread, this vivacious and vibrant wine offers instant aromatic appeal. Then the attack is authoritative, with tumbling flavors of lime zest, pea pod, and a gentle allusion of warm bread somewhere. Generous, affable, and tangy, this wine surges and lingers. Light-bodied with 12.5% ABV.

6

Other Great Whites

Although the big three varieties (Chardonnay, Pinot Grigio, and Sauvignon Blanc) are what most people drink most of the time throughout North America, white wine is also made from a wide range of other grapes—and some are swoon-worthy. In fact, peachy-pear Torrontés, lime-scented Riesling, lychee- and rose-infused Gewürztraminer, sunny Moscato, and many other varieties as well as white blends can be seriously swoon-worthy.

But you need to know which bottles are good, better, and best. This chapter offers you that candid information. It's a nod and a wink to the glorious white wines outside that tight clique of more popular grape varieties. These are wines with regional appeal, open-handed generosity of flavor, and intriguing—if less traditional—beauty. Unlike the other wines in this book, they weren't compared with one another directly but were judged on technical correctness, balance, and unabashed capacity to please.

Take my hand. Let's take a walk on the wild side.

$$ Other Great Whites

Ruffino
Orvieto Classico
UMBRIA, ITALY

This little Italian number is a great alternative to Pinot Grigio or unwooded Chardonnay with its restrained, crisp nature and captivating flavors of white flowers, white peach, grapefruit oil, and chalk, with a hint of almond on the finish. This bone-dry, elegant wine offers good value and is versatile with food. Light-bodied with 12.5% ABV.

Barefoot
Moscato
CALIFORNIA

The label is right: This wine is deliciously sweet. Aromatic flavors of wildflowers, rose, dried apricot, and sun-drenched citrus oil are balanced by a bright seam of vibrant acidity—juicy and compact. Full-bodied with 9% ABV.

**Woodbridge
Moscato**
CALIFORNIA

Sweet marmalade and stewed apricot aromas lead to lusciously sweet flavors of mixed citrus and yellow stone fruit poached in sugar. Because the sweetness is counterbalanced by invigorating acidity, it finishes clean and dry. Rich concentration, pristine fruit, and a polished mouthfeel combine to make this a good value dessert wine. Light-bodied with 9.5% ABV.

What Is Orvieto?

Orvieto is an Italian wine produced near the medieval city of the same name in Umbria. It can often be bland and uninteresting, but Ruffino's version is fragrant and fairly complex. It's based on a mix of local Grechetto, Procanico, Verdello, and Canaiolo Bianco wine grapes.

Food Pairing Tip

Pair Ruffino Orvieto Classico with crostini topped with roasted tomatoes, olive oil, and shavings of a good Parmesan cheese for a special treat.

Moscato: Great-Value Dessert Wine

Moscato can be a smart-value alternative to more expensive dessert wines. Serve it with simple pound cake, apple pie, or a selection of cheeses.

$$$ Other Great Whites

Relax
Riesling
GERMANY

The attractive sea salt and lemon blossom perfume of this pale, straw-colored wine is followed by pronounced flavors of bright lime, juicy peach, and crisp apple. Off-dry but finishes dry. This is a sleek, accessible wine. Light-bodied with 9% ABV.

Schmitt Söhne
Riesling
GERMANY

A slow-to-warm-up-to-you nose of cool steel leads to a brisk, off-dry attack of green apple and lime oil edged with that cool steeliness and slight note of kerosene often found in Riesling. Taut and intense-tasting wine with a simple classicism appreciated by those who know and love German Riesling. Light-bodied with 10% ABV.

BEST

Fetzer Gewürztraminer
MONTEREY COUNTY, CALIFORNIA

Quiet scents of ginger, rosewater, and white peach rise from the glass before orange zest, roses, ginger, and lemon-lime rush in with a kiss of sweetness offset with mouthwatering acidity. A note of crushed stone lends a bit of gravitas to the wine. Beguiling and engaging. Light- to medium-bodied with 12% ABV.

Food Pairing Tip
Riesling's lime-squirt acidity and relatively light body makes it an excellent wine to serve with spicy fare, such as Szechuan dishes, sizzling stir-fries, or even Jamaican jerk chicken.

Top Dollar
Germany is the heartland of great Riesling, with the Mosel region spinning out arguably the most admirable bottles in the world. While German Rieslings are often the bargains of the wine world today, that wasn't always the case. In the late 1800s, they fetched higher prices than top red Bordeaux, which are some of the most expensive bottles on the market today.

$$$$ Other Great Whites

Apothic White
CALIFORNIA

This plump, buttery blend of Chardonnay, Riesling, and Pinot Grigio drenches the tongue with flavors of warm praline and creamy vanilla custard—all charged with an electric citric zeal that keeps it tasting fresh and well balanced. The finish is short, but the desire to return for another sip is strong and immediate. Medium-bodied with 12.5% ABV.

M. Chapoutier
Les Vignes de Bila-Haut
COTES DU ROUSSILLON, FRANCE

Made by a respected name in winemaking, this dashing little white will have you at *bonjour*! It's tight and bright but retains that French restraint that keeps it tasting steely and stately rather than fruit-forward. Well-toned aromas and flavors of grapefruit and smoked stones draw you in and keep you stoked. Medium-bodied with 13.5% ABV.

WHITE WINES

A Word on Torrontés

Torrontés is Argentina's signature white wine variety but can be a bit flabby—which means low in acidity—putting it off balance. A way to get around this risk is to grow Torrontés at higher altitudes, which can preserve the crispness in the final wine. The Alamos featured here hails from the high-altitude vineyards in the northwestern region of Salta.

Alamos Torrontés
SALTA, ARGENTINA

Pure aromas of green pear on the nose lead to cool, crisp flavors of the same laced with lemon-lime and salt. This is a surprisingly restrained, almost austere and bone-dry style of Torrontés with much delicacy and finesse and a finely grained mineral seam. Love how the long, salivating saltiness rings on the finish. Medium-bodied with 13% ABV.

PART **3**

RED WINES

7

Red Blends

Three beauties who resemble Gosling, Tatum, and Timberlake—or Johansson, Lawrence, and Fox, if you prefer—are each obviously more than fine alone, but together, they're a fierce, light-up-the-night charm squad. It's alchemy. The halo effect. More than the sum, as it goes. And it's the same with red wine: A good blend can improve the overall package.

A coarse Cabernet Sauvignon seems smoother with Merlot. A rich, chocolaty Shiraz gets a spike of juicy freshness from Grenache. And a sassy but simple Sangiovese—the grape of Chianti—gains sophistication and complexity with a dash of Canaiolo, Cabernet Sauvignon, or even Merlot.

Blending is exciting stuff, and winemakers really get into it, manipulating more than flavor, aroma, and acidity; they play with tannin—that tongue-gripping, gum-drying quality that in the best case feels like supple, crushed velvet in the mouth. Imagine the plush vest of some eighteenth-century royal in full regalia—not that you would be pressing your tongue against it. Or maybe you would; I don't know. Point is, winemakers toy with tannins to strive for textural nirvana.

Technical stuff aside, blending boils down to one thing: better wine at better prices. Just taste a few of the bottles recommended in this chapter. You'll see.

$$ Red Blends

**Ruffino
Chianti**
TUSCANY, ITALY

Although the main grape variety in this tart cherry–scented wine is Sangiovese, it's also seasoned with other grape varieties, including Cabernet Sauvignon and Merlot. It offers a seriously tart hit of cherries on the nose and palate, with a sprinkle of earthy white pepper. Light-bodied with 12.5% ABV.

**Jacob's Creek
Classic
Shiraz Cabernet**
AUSTRALIA

Expect a smooth, swift swirl of smoky, chocolaty, berry goodness imbued with tobacco, cedar, and coffee. Then, after a moment, the smooth wash gives way to a bit of texture, with finely grained tannins creating some tug that holds the flavor in place on the finish. Good value. Full-bodied with 14.9% ABV.

BEST

Did You Know?
Although Chianti must be a minimum 80% Sangiovese, it can (and usually does) contain up to 20% of other permitted varieties.

Food Pairing Tip
Chianti is the perfect pizza wine because it's taut acidity stands up beautifully to tomato sauce, salty-fatty meats like pepperoni or sausage, and cheese.

Folonari Chianti
TUSCANY, ITALY

This delicious blend of Sangiovese, Canaiolo Nero, Trebbiano Toscano, Malvasia del Chianti, and Merlot exudes a soft talc-like perfume of dusty cherries. Understated notes of wild berries (raspberries and strawberries), crushed violet, and a touch of dried herbs taper to a talc-textured finish. Light- to medium-bodied with 13% ABV.

$$$ Red Blends

Banfi
Centine
TUSCANY, ITALY

This Sangiovese, Merlot, and Cabernet Sauvignon blend drinks like a Chianti with its bright shock of tart red cherry and earthy–peppery underpinnings. But there's not a lot else going on, making it a fairly average dry red blend. Light- to medium-bodied with 12.5% ABV.

Apothic Red
CALIFORNIA

This wildly popular wine offers tons of dark fruit layered with chocolate, vanilla, and spice. It can be a bit sweet for seasoned aficionados, but many wine drinkers like it that way. Expect a rich-tasting red with a smooth mouthfeel and no or alcoholic burn. Full-bodied with 13.5% ABV.

RED WINES

BEST

Food Pairing Tip

Cupcake Red Velvet wine is a harmonious blend of Zinfandel, Merlot, and Petite Sirah that goes fabulously well with cocoa-rubbed baby back ribs.

Cupcake Vineyards Red Velvet
CALIFORNIA

If you like red velvet cake, you'll love this wine. It starts with an unmistakable whiff of dark chocolate cake before following through with the same on the palate edged slightly with notes of vanilla and mixed berries, a whisper of black coffee, and a certain creaminess somewhere. The finish offers a little note of dry cocoa that lingers. Medium-bodied with 13.5% ABV.

$$$ Red Blends

**Alamos
Red Blend**
MENDOZA, ARGENTINA

Made from Malbec, Bonarda, and Tempranillo, this wine exudes aromas of blackberry and finely ground mixed peppercorns before gripping the palate with chewy flavors that recall cola, blackberry, dried earth, walnut skins, and cast iron. The firm tannins make it taste a bit tough relative to its competitors. Medium-bodied with 13% ABV.

**14 Hands Winery
Hot to Trot
Red Blend**
COLUMBIA VALLEY,
WASHINGTON

This blend of Merlot and Syrah tastes succulent. The ripe black cherry core unravels with compelling flavors of grilled red meat, bittersweet chocolate, caffè latte, and crushed red berries. Quite a lot of depth, power, and persistence in this hedonistic red. Medium-bodied with 13.5% ABV.

Josh Is Popular

Joseph Carr founded Josh Cellars in 2007—named after his father. Since then, the wines have soared to popularity. The Legacy Red featured here tastes amazing with a thick, juicy steak and potatoes.

Josh Cellars Legacy Red Wine
CALIFORNIA

No wonder this red blend of Merlot, Zinfandel, and Petite Sirah is popular. It's riveting! The opulent, polished fruit suggests the best-ever chocolate-covered cherries, with hints of blackberry, poached plum, blueberry pie, pipe tobacco, hazelnut, salt, and pepper—all swirling together seamlessly. Magnetic! Medium-bodied with 13.5% ABV.

$$$$ Red Blends

GOOD

BETTER

Ménage à Trois
Silk
Soft Red Blend
CALIFORNIA

Aptly named, this silky blend of Pinot Noir, Malbec and Petite Sirah swathes the palate with lit flavors of raspberry jam imbued with warm wood, cola, vanilla bean, and toasted cashew nut. It's a long, seductive wine of complexity, concentration, and character—and an unabashed kiss of sweetness. Medium-bodied with 13.5% ABV.

Ménage à Trois
California Red Wine
CALIFORNIA

This Ménage à Trois of Zinfandel, Merlot, and Cabernet Sauvignon might just turn you on with its spicy blackberry, sweet cherry, and warm cassis flavors intertwined with delicate lacings of cinnamon and raspberry jam. This is a fruit bomb that manages to maintain its composure. Medium-bodied with 13.5% ABV.

BEST

**Bogle Vineyards
Essential Red**
CALIFORNIA

This gorgeous, saturated blend of Zinfandel, Syrah, Cabernet Sauvignon, and Petite Sirah offers immediate pleasure, starting with the purest aromas of homemade blackberry jam. Then the entry is smooth and lush, with dry, cashmere flavors of macerated berries, roasted coffee bean, vanilla bean, marzipan, roasted meat, and pipe tobacco. Full-bodied with 13.5% ABV.

8

Cabernet Sauvignon

Cabernet Sauvignon (pronounced *ka-bur-NAY so-vee-NYON*) always smells and tastes of black currant. But it can be one of the most complex wines in the world, with flavors of cassis, tobacco, coffee, leather, pencil shavings, green bell pepper, grilled meat, Christmas cake, cedar, brambles, peppercorn, and more.

Sure, Bordeaux started the hype with its top Cabernet Sauvignon–based wines commanding extraordinarily high prices for well over a century. But top makers from elsewhere are certainly making some seriously fab Cab. In fact, it seems the whole world is in on the game, creating quite a competitive landscape. The glut pushes prices down and quality up, and today, there are more stellar bottles of Cabernet Sauvignon available than any other wine variety. Although the top wines from prestigious regions and properties still fetch sky-high prices, the ripple effect creates amazing values for $10—give or take a few bucks.

To do justice to this happy fact, this chapter is filled with as many good, better, and best wines as are warranted, which are quite a few. All the wines recommended here offer seriously stellar value.

$$ Cabernet Sauvignon

Concha y Toro Frontera
CHILE

This bright, juicy style of Cabernet Sauvignon will appeal to those who prefer a lighter, more lifted expression of the variety. Think wild strawberries and other tender red fruit laced with a gentle sprinkling of dark cocoa and toasted hazelnuts. After the swallow, it all tapers to black olive, coffee bean, and walnut finish. Light-bodied with 12% ABV.

Canyon Road
CALIFORNIA

Ripe, sweet aromas of raspberry jam waft effortlessly from the glass and lead to a generously fruited swirl of raspberry compote layered with dried plum and melting milk chocolate. This is a compelling, off-dry but balanced wine with an affable, easy-to-enjoy nature. Medium-bodied with 13% ABV.

Did You Know?

Cabernet Sauvignon is actually a crossing of two grape varieties: Cabernet Franc and Sauvignon Blanc—a fact only discovered in 1997 with DNA fingerprint testing conducted at the University of California at Davis.

BEST

Black Box
CHILE

Who says boxed wine can't be delicious? If in doubt, taste this. It's a well-made Cabernet Sauvignon with all the dappled complexity, dry concentration, and length of its more reputable bottled peers at a fraction of the price. Black currant, cassis, cherry, chocolate, peppercorn, and a hint of warm wood with a gentle tug of tannin on the finish combine for great value. Light-bodied with 12.5% ABV.

$$ Cabernet Sauvignon

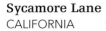

Sycamore Lane
CALIFORNIA

A fairly single-note Cabernet Sauvignon with vague flavors of black currant liqueur and warm wood with a bit of a tannic finish. It's clean and juicy but lacks the velvet mouthfeel and complexity to take it to the next level. Medium-bodied with 13.5% ABV.

Lindeman's
Bin 45
SOUTH EASTERN AUSTRALIA

Muted but pure aromas of cassis draw you toward the wash of macerated red and black berries, raspberry jam, dark chocolate, fig, toasted wood, and a dusting of crushed almonds and nutmeg. And the velvety texture and final note of caffé latte cements the idea that this wine offers delicious value for the money. Medium-bodied with 13.5% ABV.

BEST

Food Pairing Tip

Flipflop Cabernet Sauvignon pairs well with dark chocolate— especially the salted kind.

Did You Know?

The little tongue-in-cheek "LEFT COAST" on the Flipflop label is an ironic play on Bordeaux's "left bank," where some of most expensive Cabernet in the world is grown.

Flipflop
LEFT COAST, CALIFORNIA

The initial impression of homemade black cherry jam on the nose and palate quickly morphs to a slightly more serious-tasting expression with flavors of espresso, black currant liqueur, and dark chocolate quickly coming to the forefront. There's a kiss of sweetness, yes, but also a lingering coffee-cherry-nut finish. Medium-bodied with 13% ABV.

$$ Cabernet Sauvignon

[yellow tail]
SOUTH EASTERN
AUSTRALIA

You know grape popsicles? That's what this wine smells and tastes like—smooth, sweet, and candied—but with a lick of chocolate on the finish. And because the sweetness adds weight to the wine, it tastes quite fleshy and mouthcoating. Those who like it love it, which is why it's wildly popular. Full-bodied with 13.5% ABV.

Barefoot
CALIFORNIA

A big blast of berry fruit explodes on the palate, with a soft, sweet, jammy center and inflections of toasted oak expressed as baking spices—especially clove—and vanilla. The wine is a bit confected tasting but also lush and velvety, with a short but appealing blackberry aftertaste. Medium-bodied with 13.5% ABV.

> **It's a Fact**
> With more than 843,000 acres under vine in total, Cabernet Sauvignon is one of the most widely planted red wine grapes in the world. In California alone, more than 90,780 acres of that wine grape is planted.

BEST

Rex Goliath: The Giant 47 Pound Rooster
CALIFORNIA

The label doesn't lie when it says "BOLD SMOOTH FLAVOR." Expect a big, fruit-forward hit of cherry–plum goodness that's a bit one-dimensional but certainly succulent, with great texture, concentration, and purity. This is a riot of goodness that would work beautifully as a cocktail alternative. Fun to drink, off-dry, and well balanced. Medium- to full-bodied with 13% ABV.

RED WINES

$$ Cabernet Sauvignon

Beringer
Main & Vine
CALIFORNIA

Powdery scents of fresh violet, warm talc, and raspberries draw you toward a generous and pure-tasting cherry–vanilla center nuanced with coffee and toasted hazelnuts from an integrated oak influence. The finish is a bit thin and tannic, but otherwise, this is a perfectly lovely, easy-drinking bottle. Medium-bodied with 13.5% ABV.

Mezzacorona
Estate Bottled
ITALY

Light, wispy aromas of dusty cherry lead to a smooth, almost delicate expression of Cabernet Sauvignon that calls to mind violet pastilles, vanilla bean, wild blueberry, and red fruits (mostly cherry). The texture is refined with finely grained tannins, the core tastes lifted and juicy, and the length is understated but resonant. Pretty wine. Light- to medium-bodied with 13% ABV.

BEST

Did You Know?
Globally, drinkers consume 1.7 million glasses of Jacob's Creek wine every day. In fact, Jacob's Creek has the widest distribution of any Australian wine brand—it's exported to 77 countries.

What to Do With a Grippy Finish
If you find a wine is a bit too tannic for your liking, drink it with something high in protein and fat, such as steak. The fat and protein interact with the tannin to reduce the grippy feeling, enhancing the food—and the wine.

Jacob's Creek Classic
SOUTH EASTERN AUSTRALIA

This is a quick hit of sunshine in a glass. Oodles of ripe, robust berry fruit (red and black) taste plush and mouthcoating while licorice, charcoal, and fruitcake imbue the fruit core. It's all well balanced with sprightly mouthwatering acidity to keep it tasting clean and fresh. Dazzlingly good value. Full-bodied with 13.9% ABV.

$$$ Cabernet Sauvignon

RED WINES

Concha y Toro
Casillero del Diablo
Reserva
CENTRAL VALLEY, CHILE

Rich aromas of black coffee and cherries lead to a quenchingly crisp attack. Expect fairly firm tannins scaffolding flavors of cassis and coffee, cherries, and mint. This wine is bone-dry, with a bit astringency on the finish. Medium-bodied with 13.5% ABV.

Blackstone
CALIFORNIA

A sweet perfume of toasted tobacco and blackberry rise from the glass and draw you toward a polished, expansive entry. The shiny, off-dry character tastes robust and finishes dry and gently chalky. Shadowy allusions of toasted cinnamon stick and salted hazelnut lend depth and interest to an otherwise fairly simple but correct wine. Medium-bodied with 13.5% ABV.

It's a Myth

Simply opening a bottle to let it breathe does precious little for the flavor because it only exposes the surface area in the bottleneck to air. If you want to let any kind of wine breathe, decant it or pour it into stemware before serving.

BEST

Beringer Founders' Estate
CALIFORNIA

This chocolate- and cherry-scented wine tastes juicy and ripe, with traces of cassis, peppercorn, and vanilla showing through the opulent core. Finely grained, lushly textured tannins create the impression of cashmere in the mouth. Well put together wine and outstanding value for the money. Full-bodied with 13.8% ABV.

$$$ Cabernet Sauvignon

Santa Rita
120 Reserva Especial
CENTRAL VALLEY, CHILE

This bone-dry and relatively austere style of Cabernet Sauvignon shows cherries and dry pencil shavings on the nose and palate, with a walnut-skin drying sensation on the long black tea finish. Medium-bodied with 13% ABV.

Dark Horse
The Original
CALIFORNIA

Subdued aromas of cola and cassis lead to a sleek, satiny entry that quickly fans out to suggest sweet cherries and black currant underpinned with warm wood, cola, and cassis. Quite a dry, relatively serious-tasting wine for the money, with a touch of tapenade on the finish. Medium-bodied with 13.5% ABV.

Cabernet Sauvignon $$$

RED WINES

BEST

It's a Fact
Cabernet Sauvignon grapes are small and blue rather than the black or purple color of most other red wine grapes. Their thick skins and low skin-to-juice ratio impart considerable color, flavor, and tannin to the wine.

Wine Tip
A cork's throw away from California on the map, Washington is fast becoming an exciting place to look for sun-drenched, complex styles of Cabernet Sauvignon.

Columbia Crest Grand Estates
COLUMBIA VALLEY, WASHINGTON

Wild blueberries and smoky oak aromas lead to a mouth-filling crush of dark berries with lots of depth underneath: creamy vanilla, milk chocolate, coal, coffee, earth, leather, and anise. A suave, sophisticated, and undervalued wine with finely grained, ripe tannins that feel like velvet. Full-bodied with 13.5% ABV.

$$$ Cabernet Sauvignon

Fetzer
Valley Oaks
CALIFORNIA

Aromas of black currant, red licorice, and chalk draw you toward a smooth, sweet, surge of tart cherries, mocha, cassis, charcoal, and dried herbs, with a certain salinity lacing the tart–sweet fruit. A bit of puckering astringency on the finish is a little anticlimactic though. Full-bodied with 13.5% ABV.

Smoking Loon
The Original
CENTRAL VALLEY, CHILE

Such a rich hit of goodness! Each sip offers rippling cassis, black cherry, grilled meat, dried currants, cappuccino, chocolate shavings, and smoky charcoal flavors that lead to a slightly chalky finish. Great wine for the money. Medium-bodied with 13.5% ABV.

BEST

Who Drinks the Most Cabernet Sauvignon?

The two biggest markets for Cabernet Sauvignon are mainland China and the United States.

19 Crimes
LIMESTONE COAST, AUSTRALIA

With thunderclap intensity, this wine explodes with dark fruit flavors—blueberries, blackberries, dried plum, and sultanas. Then, after the initial attack, it continues to unfurl considerable complexity—fruitcake, cigar box, pencil shavings, mint, gravel, and espresso notes that linger. Big, bold and brawny expression with a velvet mouthfeel. Incredible value. Full-bodied with 14% ABV.

$$$$ Cabernet Sauvignon

Santa Rita Reserva
MAIPO VALLEY, CHILE

Ripe raspberry flavors taste bright and arresting, with waves of melted chocolate running through the shock of tart fruit. Somewhat balanced, but it could use a bit more ripeness and concentration. On the finish, an astringent note of black tea tugs at the gums. Not a terribly typical style but enough varietal character to taste correct. Medium-bodied with 13.5% ABV.

Chateau St. Jean
CALIFORNIA

Barely there aromas of red meat and cassis lead to a refined, restrained style of Cabernet Sauvignon. Muted flavors of dried cherry, cassis, crushed stones, salt, dried herbs, and warm, toasted wood come together in an intriguing tapestry that tastes equally classic and clearly defined. Considerable poise and elegance here. Full-bodied with 13.8% ABV.

BEST

Toasted Head Barrel Aged
CALIFORNIA

Black cherry aromas lead to a surging, lip-smacking wash of dark cherry imbued with toffee, toasted marshmallow, creamy vanilla, and a certain graham cracker toastiness somewhere. The rich but breezy entry offers pure pleasure, which endures through the resonant finish. Absolutely a wine with attitude to burn. Medium-bodied with 13.5% ABV.

$$$$ Cabernet Sauvignon

Carnivor
CALIFORNIA

Tasting almost spoonable, this plush Cabernet Sauvignon is definitely one that will appeal to those looking for a mighty, mouthcoating red. Expect intense flavors of blueberry jam, cassis, melting chocolate, and toasted oak supported by a firm, muscular structure. Full-bodied with 14% ABV.

Chateau Souverain
CALIFORNIA

Warm aromas of stewed raspberries with a hint of mint lead to a swell of plush-tasting elegance. Stewed raspberries drizzled with dark chocolate, a touch of vanilla bean, and a sprinkle of toasted hazelnuts—it's all here. The finish is a bit short but otherwise, it's a well-made and delicious bottle of red wine. Full-bodied with 13.9% ABV.

BEST

The Story Behind Carnivor Wine

This wine was designed specifically for men. After doing a ton of market research, winemakers learned guys want a wine that's flavorful and robust, bold and smooth, and not too dry. They want one that signals manliness. They want to look at it on the shelf and immediately know they can serve it with a great steak. Voilà! Carnivor was born in all its stereotypical grunting glory.

14 Hands Winery
COLUMBIA VALLEY, WASHINGTON

A seductive, warm berry perfume draws you in. Then intense flavors of macerated cherries and blueberries stitched with black earth, toasted almond, nutmeg, and clove notes offer depth while the plunging acidity and plush tannins hold the fruit in place. This is an iron-fisted, velvet-gloved wine of personality and substance. Medium- to full-bodied with 13.5% ABV.

$$$$ Cabernet Sauvignon

Columbia Winery
COLUMBIA VALLEY,
WASHINGTON

Pronounced perfume of warm red licorice is clear as day and leads to more of the same on the palate that tapers to a tea and walnut skin finish. A bit simple and confected on the palate and slightly astringent on the finish. Full-bodied with 13.7% ABV.

Noble Vines Collection 337
LODI, CALIFORNIA

Grilled peppercorn steak aromas lead to a bright wash of cranberries stewed with allspice and clove and drizzled with cassis. Then the smoky–spicy notes of grilled peppercorn steak come back to linger on the finish. This wine has a chunky, slightly chewy structure but is ripe and well made. Full-bodied with 14% ABV.

Cabernet Sauvignon **$$$$**

BEST

Estancia Vineyards
PASO ROBLES, CALIFORNIA

Lovely, powdery scents of talc, dried currants, and black cherry lead to a classy and smart-tasting expression. Layered flavors of red berries, damson, cocoa, violet petals, cassis, sage, and warm gravel unspool slowly. Then the finish leaves a discreet note of salt, sage, and stone. Doesn't drink like an under-$15 bottle! Medium-bodied with 13.5% ABV.

Napa Beats Bordeaux!

In 1976, in Paris, France, top Cabernet Sauvignon-based wines from Napa Valley were tasted blind against those of Bordeaux by leading critics. The event was called the Judgment of Paris and the results shocked and shook the wine world. When the scores were tallied, a Californian Cabernet came out on top: The 1973 Stag's Leap Wine Cellars Cabernet Sauvignon won first.

$$$$ Cabernet Sauvignon

Sterling Vintner's Collection
CALIFORNIA

Classic scents of cassis rise from the glass before the smooth entry calls to mind Grandma's bumbleberry pie—bright, baked fruit and toasted pastry. The sip soon tapers to a slight tug on the finish, along with a note of violet and caramelized sugar. Medium-bodied with 13.5% ABV.

Alamos
MENDOZA, ARGENTINA

This rich but refreshing Cabernet Sauvignon is chockful of blueberry and blackberry liqueur flavors edged with graphite and lit with a bright, spiraling cherry–almond delicacy. Such an exciting balance of full-fruited appeal and lifted elegance from Argentina. Medium-bodied with 13% ABV.

BEST

Columbia Crest
H3
HORSE HEAVEN HILLS,
WASHINGTON

This offers more concentration, complexity, and length than most under-$15 Cabs. Lashings of super-ripe red and black berries laced with warm cocoa, granite, toasted oak, charcoal, black tea, and red and black licorice rivet the senses. The length lingers with a twist of cherry and vanilla on the finish. Full-bodied with 14.5% ABV.

Mountains Matter
The mountains depicted on the label of Alamos Cabernet Sauvignon pay homage to the fact that growing grapes at higher altitudes can preserve freshness and elegance in a wine—without compromising flavor. This particular bottle is made from grapes grown 3,000 to 5,000 feet above sea level.

CONSISTENT QUALITY, PROVEN VALUE

BAREFOOT

MOST AWARDED

WINE BRAND

U.S. COMPETITIONS

BAREFOOT.

MERLOT

CALIFORNIA

ALC 13% BY VOL.

9

Merlot

If you like plump, lush cherries dunked in melted chocolate, you'll probably like well-made Merlot (pronounced *mer-LOW*) because that's essentially what it tastes like. In best cases, it's the smoothest, most supple, and most accessible of all reds.

If Cabernet Sauvignon is power, then Merlot is finesse. If Pinot Noir is complex and challenging, then Merlot is relatively straightforward and easy to enjoy. That said, Merlot has suffered an image problem since about 2004, when wine snob Miles Raymond uttered these now famous words in the hit film *Sideways*: "No, if anyone orders Merlot, I'm leaving. I am NOT drinking any fucking Merlot!"

Sideways scored 96% on Rotten Tomatoes with its amusing and allusive tale of two mixed-up, middle-aged guys on a road trip through Californian wine country. Main character Miles's love for Pinot Noir and hatred for Merlot affected these wine styles in the real world too: Merlot became less popular and Pinot Noir sales soared. (The fact that Miles's all-time favorite wine, Cheval Blanc, is about half Merlot was lost on most viewers.)

All this matters because the so-called "*Sideways* Effect" (search Google—it's a thing) forced Merlot producers to up their game. Now more than a decade later, Merlot has never been better. Need proof? Taste some wines described in this chapter.

$$ Merlot

[yellow tail]
SOUTH EASTERN
AUSTRALIA

Port-like aromas of stewed black forest fruits and fig lead to a full-on, dry-tasting display of ripe, stewed berries and black plums drizzled with milk chocolate. Then, on the finish, white chocolate emerges and lingers. A soft, supple, lush wine with a sweet center that finishes dry. Full-bodied with 13.5% ABV.

**Woodbridge
by Robert Mondavi**
CALIFORNIA

Smooth and balanced red with juicy aromas and flavors of black cherry, blackberry, cedar, black peppercorn, and a light sifting of soft cocoa powder. A mellow midweek quaffer with a long, attractively chalky finish that holds the fruit in place nicely. Medium-bodied with 13.5% ABV.

BEST

Barefoot
CALIFORNIA

Aromas of homemade blueberry pie lead to a dry but not bone-dry attack of sun-drenched black and red cherry, wild blueberry, raspberry, and dark chocolate—one fell swoop of sure-fire satisfaction with a long dark cocoa powder finish. Unassuming little bottle of liquid thrill factor. Full-bodied with 13.5% ABV.

What to Do With Leftover Barefoot?

Make brownies with this adaptation from the winery's recipe:

Ingredients
4oz dark chocolate, chopped
½ cup butter, cut into pieces
¼ cup Barefoot Merlot
2 eggs, at room temperature
¾ cup white sugar
1 tsp vanilla
½ cup all-purpose flour
¼ cup unsweetened cocoa powder
½ tsp kosher salt

For the glaze
2oz semisweet chocolate
1 tbsp unsalted butter
2 tbsp Barefoot Merlot

Directions
1. Preheat oven to 350°F (177°C).
2. On the stovetop, in a small pot over low heat, melt chocolate and butter until smooth. Whisk in wine until fully incorporated.
3. Remove the pot from the heat, and whisk in eggs one at a time.
4. Stir in sugar and vanilla, then add flour, cocoa powder, and salt, and stir until smooth.
5. Transfer to a 9" x 9" foil-lined pan and bake for 25 minutes.
6. To make the glaze, on the stovetop, in a small pot over low heat, melt chocolate and butter until smooth. Whisk in wine.
7. When the brownies are cool, drizzle the glaze over top and spread it using an offset spatula.

$$$ Merlot

Fetzer
Eagle Peak
CALIFORNIA

This pure-fruited Merlot starts with captivating aromas of cherry cola and vanilla before sliding over the palate with velvety-crisp flavors of the same framed with warm toffee and a gentle mix of dried bay leaf and rubbed oregano. As the wine recedes, a slightly astringent grip and a clear-as-a-bell note of black olive emerges and lingers. Full-bodied with 13.5% ABV.

Bogle Vineyards
CALIFORNIA

Lots of creamy, toasty vanilla oak underpin ripe cherry, spicy pipe tobacco, and melted chocolate on the nose and palate. Not only is the flavor profile compelling, but the structure is too; it tastes tightly wound, juicy, and mouth-filling before tapering to a long finish tinged with toasted nuts and coffee. Stylish. Full-bodied with 13.5% ABV.

Food Pairing Tip
Merlot goes well with many foods, but it's particularly stellar with herb-crusted pork chops, roasted chicken, and grilled pizza.

BEST

Columbia Crest Grand Estates
COLUMBIA VALLEY, WASHINGTON

Warm chocolate cake and blackberry aromas lead to an opulent palate of dried plum, black and red poached berries, and chocolate cake again—with a chocolate mousse mouthfeel. This quite dense yet suave wine with an artisanal, "crafted," not "produced" air about it is serious juice at a surprisingly low price. Full-bodied with 13.5% ABV.

$$$$ Merlot

Robert Mondavi Private Selection
CALIFORNIA

This jammy Merlot exudes rich aromas of stewed black cherries before sliding across the palate with robust flavors of black cherry jam, chocolate-covered raisins, dried plum, and fruitcake. Quite a complex wine. Full-bodied with 13.5% ABV.

14 Hands Winery
COLUMBIA VALLEY, WASHINGTON

While the nose is rather shy and vaguely berry-like, the entry rivets with depth and power, creamy finesse, and a long gleaming length. Flavors of wild cherries dunked in chocolate, Grandma's blueberry tarts, and strokes of cola and vanilla attack before crashing into a short dark chocolate and black cherry finish with a final note of black earth. Full-bodied with 13.5% ABV.

A Little History
Merlot came to California in the mid-nineteenth century and is now one of the leading red wines sold in the United States.

J. Lohr
Los Osos
PASO ROBLES, CALIFORNIA

Precise aromas of raspberry jam, prune, and blueberry lead to an enticingly complex palate of raspberry jam layered with blackberry, prune, turned earth, damp stones, cedar, tobacco leaf, tar, and sweet spice. The cashmere mouthfeel lends depth to the expression. This stylish Merlot tastes like a wine worth more than its price. Full-bodied with 13.5% ABV.

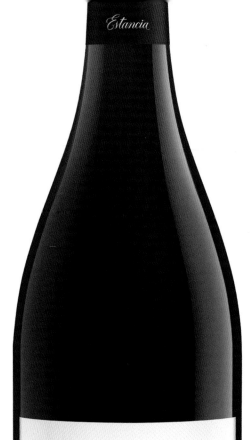

Estancia

GROWN WITH PASSION

PINOT NOIR
MONTEREY COUNTY

10

Pinot Noir

Pinot Noir (pronounced *pee-no NWAHR*) tastes of strawberry, raspberry, cranberry, cherry, and violet. After a while in the bottle, it shifts toward flavors of beets, underbrush, and barnyard—nuances that give it an earthy, almost primal appeal.

Pinot Noir is a relatively light, smooth, refreshing red that can be incredibly complex and beguiling. In fact, before the 2004 movie *Sideways*, Pinot-philes were like a secret sect of hardcore oenophiles sharing their private passion for this variety, which can make silky wines of drop-dead elegance—seriously seductive stuff.

Then *Sideways* blew the club wide open. Almost everyone who saw the film flocked to taste this holy grail of red wine. Winemakers in California, referring to the "*Sideways* Effect," responded swiftly by cutting Merlot vines off at the trunk and grafting on Pinot Noir.

Ever since, everyone wants in on the game, and winemakers are churning out Pinot Noir everywhere—from the United States to Australia. As winemakers toil away in the vineyards and wineries to capture the elusive thrill of Pinot Noir, some really good versions are hitting shelves at much more affordable prices than those fine-caliber—but expensive—gems from the variety's heartland of Burgundy, France. To see what I mean, just taste some of the wines recommended in this chapter.

$$ Pinot Noir

Stemmari
SICILY, ITALY

Barely there aromas of blackberry lead to a crisp entry of mixed red berries. Ripe yet elegant expression from Sicily, with a hint of crushed pink and black peppercorn on the finish. Light- to medium-bodied with 13% ABV.

Mezzacorona Estate Bottled
DOLOMITI, ITALY

Dusty cherry flavors make this initially taste more like a Chianti than a Pinot Noir. Expect a light, lively entry with oodles of mouthwatering acidity, a pure fruit center, and an attractively chalky finish. Light- to medium-bodied with 13% ABV.

Food Pairing Tip

Pinot Noir is a perfect match for grilled salmon, roasted poultry, lamb, or ham. It also works well with the French stew called cassoulet, especially when the wine is made in the more restrained Burgundian style.

Folonari
ITALY

A slow, languid fragrance of violet and raspberry rises from this pale wine. Then the attack is bright but not shrill, with delicate floral–berry flavors edged with soft earth and dried cranberry. The seamless structure, lacquered mouthfeel, and long finish are earmarks of fine craftsmanship. Light-bodied with 12.5% ABV.

$$$ Pinot Noir

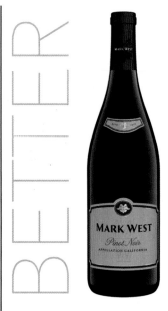

Mirassou Winery
CALIFORNIA

This Californian beauty offers fragrant floral and red berry fruit on the nose; a sleek, quenching entry; and juicy flavors of wild blueberry, crushed violet, and fresh raspberry edged with a touch of beetroot and chalk. Easy crowd-pleaser. Medium-bodied with 13.5% ABV.

Mark West
SONOMA COUNTY, CALIFORNIA

What a delicious wine! Aromatic flavors of raspberries, violets, vanilla, and clove characterize this richly fruited, seductive Pinot Noir with resonating length. Along with considerable concentration, this wine feels silky yet well structured in the mouth, with taut acidity and soft, supple tannins. Such finesse! Full-bodied with 13.8% ABV.

Gnarly Head
CALIFORNIA

Although this is richer and more meaty tasting than most Pinot Noir, it's got instant appeal. It starts with black raspberry aromas, along with warm mocha, before exploding with voluptuous flavors of poached plum, raspberry preserves, black pepper, and charred wood. Powerful and dense style of Pinot Noir with a satisfying raspberry–vanilla finish. Full-bodied with 13.5% ABV.

A Bit of History

The Mirassou family has been growing wine grapes in sunny California since 1854, earning it the distinction of being the oldest winemaking family in the United States.

A Bit More History

Pinot Noir is ancient. It was known to the Romans in 100 AD and was cultivated in Burgundy, France, as early as the fourth century AD.

RED WINES

135

$$$$ Pinot Noir

Noble Vines Collection 667
MONTEREY, CALIFORNIA.

Almost no aroma at all exudes from this wine, but then it glides across the palate with a tight-fisted expression that suggests barely ripe strawberries and raspberries, tart cranberry, and a long puff of smoke on the finish. Full-bodied with 14.5% ABV.

Oyster Bay
MARLBOROUGH, NEW ZEALAND

A satiny-smooth Pinot with a crush of raspberries, strawberries, and cherries that unspools slowly toward a resonant finish of the same edged with a touch of oak. Supple, quenching, and well made. Medium-bodied with 13.5% ABV.

Estancia Vineyards
MONTEREY COUNTY, CALIFORNIA

A beautifully heady nose of gently smoked cherries and violet carries through with billowy flavors of cherry pound cake and tart raspberries that collapse quickly to a slightly short finish. Clean and fresh with a certain sweet creaminess going on. Medium-bodied with 13.5% ABV.

It's a Fact
Pinot Noir is one of the world's most challenging vine varieties with which to make wine. It mutates easily, is susceptible to disease, and yields thin, pale, acerbic wine if the winemaker isn't careful or if the vines are grown in unsuitable places. This means it's high risk for winemakers and drinkers alike. But when it's done well, it's incredible.

What's It Worth?
Pinot Noir is a grape full of promise—and no one delivers on that promise like wines from Domaine de la Romanée-Conti, the revered estate in Burgundy against which all other Pinot Noir is judged. In 2017, Christie's sold a 12-bottle case of 1988 Domaine de la Romanée-Conti for £198,000 (about $278,000 USD). The fact that this property's wines fetch such prices is a testament to how amazing Pinot Noir can be. I've been fortunate to taste some of these wines and can assure you that they're spellbinding.

GNARLY HEAD

BOLD SOPHISTICATED WINE

OLD VINE ZIN
LODI ZINFANDEL

11

Other Great Reds

Cabernet Sauvignon, Merlot, and Pinot Noir. You know them. You love them. And these varietals account for a large portion of the red wines made and drunk in the United States, so they each deserve an entire chapter in this book. But they don't tell the whole story.

Hundreds of wine grapes exist beyond this trio—many of which enjoy a certain level of well-deserved popularity in the United States and elsewhere. Quite frankly, this book would be remiss to exclude the thunderclap red Zinfandels and Petite Sirahs of California; tightly knit Malbecs of Argentina; bell pepper–scented Carménères of Chile; and the choco–berry Shirazes of Australia, to name just a handful. Many of these wines could command two times their prices if their grape varieties were more prestigious.

This chapter honors the best wines beyond the famous three.

$$ Other Great Reds

Barefoot Zinfandel
LODI, CALIFORNIA

This sweet-centered red offers port-like intensity and flavors of mixed berries stewed in sugar and laced with toasted oak and warm, creamy vanilla notes. Full- bodied with 13.5% ABV.

[yellow tail] Shiraz
SOUTH EASTERN AUSTRALIA

The nose needs a little coaxing, but the palate offers an instantly vibrant hit of grape jelly laced with blueberries, raspberries, and spice. Essentially, this swirl of wine tastes like alcoholic fruit juice with tons of sweet ripe fruit, except for the whispers of appealing earthiness on the finish that lend a bit of gravitas to the experience. Full-bodied with 13.0% ABV.

BEST

Lindeman's Bin 50 Shiraz
SOUTH EASTERN AUSTRALIA

The initial thunderclap hit of poached plum, wild blueberry, and milk chocolate gives way to layered complexity as clove, wet stones, cola, and salted grilled meat emerge through the ripe fruit. Quite a lot of complexity and dry, brawny concentration for the money. Long, dark chocolate finish. Full-bodied with 13.5% ABV.

Food Pairing Tip
Match Lindeman's Bin 50 Shiraz with spaghetti cacio e pepe, the classic Italian dish that tosses pasta with olive oil, butter, ground black pepper, and grated pecorino or Parmesan, for a pairing that works marvelously well.

Syrah or Shiraz?
Syrah (pronounced *see-RAH*) is a tightly wound wine that tends to taste of blackberries, blueberries, meat, black pepper, and smoke. Shiraz (pronounced *shir-AHZ*), the Australian version of the same grape, tends to be less savory, with a slightly sweeter, riper, dark chocolate character.

History Lesson
Although there are many theories as to Syrah's origin, DNA testing confirmed in 1998 that the variety originated in France's northern Rhône region and might have been around since 77 AD.

$$$ Other Great Reds

Manischewitz Blackberry
NEW YORK

This pure blackberry wine tastes just like blackberry jam in a glass—but liquefied and gourmet—with a firm alcoholic backbone sustaining the vinosity. It's lusciously sweet, with terrific purity of fruit and a bit of zippy acidity to keep it tasting fresh and sprightly. Medium-bodied with 10.5% ABV.

Manischewitz Concord Grape
NEW YORK

If you've ever tasted Welch's grape jelly, you'll know exactly what this wine tastes like—except with a kick almost totally hidden beneath the jelly jar goodness. This is a sweet wine, make no mistake, but it's well balanced by mouthwatering acidity. Kinda makes you crave a peanut butter sandwich! Medium-bodied with 10.5% ABV.

RED WINES

Jacob's Creek Classic Shiraz
SOUTH EASTERN AUSTRALIA

Explosive flavors and aromas of black plum purée, blackberry, earth, jam, charcoal, and peppercorn flood the senses. This is a robust and untamed blockbuster with no hard edges and a lush mouthfeel. It's so dense that it almost tastes spoonable. Full-bodied with 13.9% ABV.

$$$ Other Great Reds

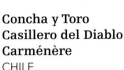

Concha y Toro
Casillero del Diablo
Carménère
CHILE

With invigorating flavors and aromas of freshly cut green peppers, mixed berries, and juicy plums nuanced with cigar, bitter chocolate, vanilla, and coffee, this is textbook Carménère with impeccable balance. Elegant, fine tannins give structure to the fruit. I particularly like the long mocha finish. Full-bodied with 13.5% ABV.

Smoking Loon
The Original
Old Vine Zinfandel
CALIFORNIA

This wine erupts with satisfyingly rich flavors of black cherry, dark chocolate shavings, wild blueberry, blackberry jam, and a good crank of black pepper—all captured in a smooth, structured whole with a glossy mouthfeel. An exciting wine for the money. Full-bodied with 14% ABV.

Carménère is ...

... the flagship winegrape of Chile. In Chile, Carménère (pronounced *car-men-AIR*) produces a deeply ruby-colored wine with a cherry–plum flavor nuanced with green pepper and sometimes notes of chocolate and violet. Carménère is originally from Bordeaux, where it can be used to add complexity to the red wines of Médoc.

**Gnarly Head
Old Vine Zinfandel**
LODI, CALIFORNIA

Expect muscular but articulate flavors of macerated blackberries and black cherry edged with black pepper, black earth, toasted tobacco, warm clove, allspice, smoke, and oak. Definitely a smart wine with swagger. Lush. Full-bodied with 14.5% ABV.

145

$$$$ Other Great Reds

Bogle Vineyards
Petite Sirah
CALIFORNIA

Aromas and flavors of super-ripe cherries, butter pound cake, and vanilla custard whirl around in this fleshy, ripe, and expansive wine. The textural dimension is firm and drying, with a grippy tug on the finish. Full-bodied with 13.5% ABV.

J. Lohr
Syrah
PASO ROBLES, CALIFORNIA

Quiet scents of summer berries on the nose lead to long, reflective flavors of strawberry jam, boysenberry, fresh fig, orange peel, cherry, and spice, with a saline undertow of green olive. Time spent in French and American oak is felt as a warm complexity that permeates the plump, plush fruit. Full-bodied with 13.5% ABV.

**Alamos
Malbec**
MENDOZA, ARGENTINA

Here's a brilliant version of Malbec at an incredible price. It delivers dense notes of plum purée, blueberry, and blackberry liqueur edged with graphite, black licorice, black pepper, tar, leather, and roses. It's complex and smooth, and all that brawny goodness is lifted with bright cherry–almond delicacy. Full-bodied with 13.% ABV.

Petite Sirah

Petite Sirah (pronounced *pe-TEET see-RAH*) makes a rich wine laden with dark berry fruit and black peppercorn. In fact, it's a cross between Syrah and Peloursin, a minor Rhône grape. Petite Sirah is darker in color and firmer in structure than Syrah or Shiraz.

Malbec

Malbec (pronounced *MAL-beck*) is a dense, inky-dark wine brimming with flavors and aromas of blackberry and dark plum, framed by a smooth but firm structure. It's the flagship red variety of Argentina. And stylistically, these wines range from ripe, round fruit-bombs to elegant, almost austere expressions of stone and fruit.

$$$$ Other Great Reds

Roscato Rosso Dolce (Sweet Red)
ITALY

This sweet, gently fizzy wine has soared in popularity in recent years—and it's understandable. Its succulent aromas of mixed berries shot through with a shock of balancing acidity and tiny bubbles offer an easy style of wine to pour anywhere anytime. Light-bodied with 7% ABV.

Carnivor Zinfandel
CALIFORNIA

Expect robust, sweet-fruited flavors of black cherries and cream layered with sweet raspberry, baking spices, warm mocha, and vanilla. A satin texture, jammy ripeness, and dense mouthfeel make this an easy win for those who want a big, bold red that's not too dry. Full-bodied with 14.5% ABV.

BEST

Concannon
Petite Sirah
LIVERMORE VALLEY,
CALIFORNIA

This interesting wine flits from black cherry to red plum, cocoa to mocha, white pepper to clove. A bright seam of mouthwatering acidity gives a bit of levity to the wine's inherent heaviness and firm structure. A rather serious-tasting wine with a long and languid finish. And definitely well worth the money! Full-bodied with 13.5% ABV.

Zinfandel is ...

... a rich red wine with deep color, full body, and high alcohol. Pronounced *ZIN-fan-dell*, it tastes of ripe, juicy blackberries and raspberries edged with black pepper—and in California, Zinfandel found its niche. Not only are the growing conditions ideal for this grape, but the wine perfectly suits American cuisine. The massive weight and peppery richness match all-American fare, like burgers, barbecue, ribs, grilled steak, and chili.

Roscato Rosso Dolce: Perfect for picnics!

Proper picnic packing starts with wine. It should be light-bodied, refreshing, and unpretentious—pompous in the park just doesn't work. Which is why Roscato Rosso Dolce is a great choice. It's low in alcohol, fizzy, and refreshing—with the perfect balance of sweet, berry freshness and tart, mouthwatering appeal. A great complement to almost anything else you tuck in the basket.

PART **4**

ROSÉ AND SPARKLING WINES

UNCORK
FOR CHANCE TO
WIN

750+
AWARDS
WON BY BERINGER

BERINGER

MAIN & VINE™

ESTABLISHED
1876

WHITE
ZINFANDEL

12

Rosé

Scantily clad French folk quaff it on the beaches of the Côte d'Azur. Euro-version "it" girls sip it in the stylish tapas bars of Spain. And fashionistas enjoy it in beachside eateries from Malibu to Miami. Frankly, in places where rosé is de rigueur, the wine is drunk rather than discussed because focus lies elsewhere—on tanned skin, on the view of the ocean, on easy afternoon chitchat—and the wet stuff in the glass merely lubricates and amplifies the moments.

In these and other major markets, rosé consumption is soaring. In France, it even overtook white wine recently in terms of sales volumes for the first time. Pink is huge. Clearly, drinking rosé isn't something to blush about. And that holds true for women as well as men. Even *GQ* magazine declared that men are in the throes of a raging bromance with "brosé." What's driving this trend is the recognition that because rosé can be a dry and complex badge of sophistication, drinking it is smart regardless of gender.

Curiously, there are many under-$7.99 wines and a few $11–$15 ones worth noting in this chapter—but not a lot in between. Thus, the midrange price bracket ($8–$10.99) has been omitted. Do trade up, though, because that upper bracket offers a lot of bottled pleasure for the money.

$$ Rosé

**Barefoot
Pink Moscato**
CALIFORNIA

Exuding aromas of kiwi fruit and juicy nectarine, this pale pink with deep coral inflections is immediately enticing. Then it douses the palate with succulent flavors of ultra-ripe nectarine, pomegranate, and maraschino cherries. Its richness could be offset with a bit more palate-cleansing acidity for balance. Light- to medium-bodied with 9% ABV.

**Barefoot
Red Moscato**
CALIFORNIA

This deep fuschia-toned rosé smells confected—much like homemade cherry pie—and ripples with lusciously sweet flavors of homemade cherry pie laced with lemon-squirt acidity. Because the bright acidity ensures perfect balance, it finishes clean and dry. Light- to medium-bodied with 9% ABV.

Sweetness and Body

Although there's usually a direct relationship between alcohol level and body—with lower alcohol resulting in lighter structure and mouthfeel—sugar changes the game. When a wine is high in sugar, as is the case with many of the wines in this chapter, it adds weight to the wine.

Making Pink Wines

Pink wines are made by letting the color-laden skins of red grapes remain with the juice briefly—after the fruit is crushed—to impart extra flavor, aroma, and color to the wine. Occasionally, though, it's made by mixing red wine with white wine.

BEST

Barefoot Rosé
CALIFORNIA

Shining the palest shade of eraser pink, this wine tastes light and airy, with wispy flavors of watermelon and sugared pink grapefruit that lingers on the finish. Beautiful balance of gentle sweetness and mouthwatering acidity ensures this rosé keeps refreshing sip after sip. A casual and slightly sweeter take on the spirit of Provencal-style rosé. Light-bodied with 10% ABV.

$$ Rosé

Sutter Home
White Zinfandel
CALIFORNIA

This is the best-selling White Zin in the United States, and it's easy to see why. Gleaming silvery-pink in the glass, the peach, orange, cantaloupe, and subtle strawberry flavors are delicate and off-dry with a good edge of incising acidity. Light-bodied with 9.5% ABV.

Barefoot
White Zinfandel
CALIFORNIA

Shatteringly fresh like a summer rainfall, this pinky-orange, off-dry wine with a slight spritz and sweet watermelon aromas washes over the tongue with flavors of rosewater, sweet pineapple, fresh orange, ripe pear, and cantaloupe. A slight astringency shows on the finish, which adds interest and appeal. Light-bodied with 9% ABV.

Beringer
White Zinfandel
CALIFORNIA

This coral rose–colored wine
with aromas of strawberry and
peach attacks the palate with a
soft shock of ripe berries and
stone fruit. It tastes bright,
concentrated, and off-dry with a
tart seam of acidity, making it an
excellent thirst-quencher. Juicy.
Light-bodied with 10% ABV.

It's a Fact
White Zinfandel was
created accidentally at
Sutter Home Winery. To
increase concentration in
the maker's red Zinfandel
wines in the 1970s, Sutter
Home extracted juice
early in the winemaking
process and used it to
make a dry so-called
White Zinfandel. In 1975,
a batch of this White
Zinfandel stopped
fermenting before the
yeast had consumed all
the sugar, leaving a wine
that was light in alcohol
and sweet. Tasting it later,
the winemaker liked it,
bottled it, and tried to
sell it. It was a huge hit,
and the style remains
popular today.

ROSÉ AND SPARKLING WINES

$$$$ Rosé

Kim Crawford Rosé
HAWK'S BAY,
NEW ZEALAND

This is a big, dry-tasting hit of berry goodness. Not a lot of complexity or nuance going on, but it definitely offers the full-throttle zip for which New Zealand has come to be known. Medium-bodied with 13.5% ABV.

Josh Cellars Rosé
CALIFORNIA

A faint fragrance of white flowers, violets, and wild strawberries draw you toward the dry, coy attack. Expect a grapefruit and white peach core laced with gentle strawberries and white flowers, a certain salinity that makes the mouth water, and a touch of nut and nougat on the finish. Tantalizing. Light-bodied with 12% ABV.

Roscato
Rosé Dolce (Sweet Rosé)
ITALY

Pale pink and gently fizzy, this wine is soaring in popularity. Its restrained aromas gently reminiscent of grapefruit zest suggest a bit of Euro-chic coyness rather than flamboyant exuberance. The light tickle of effervescence threads delicate fruit that subtly suggests berries, stone fruit, mixed citrus zest, and honey. Off-dry and delicious. Light-bodied with 8% ABV.

13

Sparkling Wine

It's easy to think of sparkling wine as alcoholic pop or toast tipple. But it's wine. With bubbles. And like all wine, its responsibility is to yield concentration, complexity, and balance. Sure, the style requires it to be lighter than average still wine, but it should retain the essential hallmarks of a fine wine. Bubbles are secondary.

And like still wine, the best bubblies make polished aperitifs while holding their own at the dinner table—the two roles that have never really been shed in Europe. Let's face it: Persistent bubbles beading up through a stemmed glass lend sparkle to any occasion.

In case you're wondering why I'm not using the term Champagne to describe sparkling wine, it's because Champagne is a wine made in the region of the same name in northern France. The term is sometimes used for sparkling wines made in the style of Champagne, but this copycat labeling bugs the French. After much lobbying, the United States banned the use of the word "Champagne" from wines made in the States. However, wines that gained approval to use the term before 2006 can continue to do that; thus, Champagne still appears on some US wine labels.

Controversial names notwithstanding, you'll find some excellent US "Champagnes" in this chapter that are more affordable than their French counterparts as well as some stellar sparkling wines from Italy, Spain, and Australia.

$$ Sparkling Wines

André
Brut
CALIFORNIA

This is a sparkling wine for apple lovers. Expect a robust hit of baked apples and not a lot else going on. Lovely lift and texture though. While this is André's least-sweet offering, it's far from bone-dry. Light-bodied with 10.5% ABV.

Cook's
Brut
CALIFORNIA

This decent-value sparkling wine has restrained aromas of green pear and lime zest. Soft sweetness hovers behind taut fruit. A well-balanced, elegant bubbly for the price. Light-bodied with 11.5% ABV.

BEST

André
Brut Rosé
CALIFORNIA

Attractively coy suggestions of freshly picked strawberries and sliced peaches rise aromatically from the glass before a juicy hit of stone fruit and berries washes over the palate. The wine is fruity but more allusive than forward in character—and that restraint spells elegance. Definitely the best value at this price. Light-bodied with 10.5% ABV.

How Sweet It Is

For sparkling wines, the following terms can appear on labels to indicate increasing levels of sweetness:

- extra brut (bone-dry)
- brut (dry)
- extra-dry (off-dry)
- sec (medium dry)
- demi-sec (medium sweet)
- doux (sweet)
- moelleux (very sweet)

Aside from the fact that extra-dry is confusingly sweeter than brut, it's all logical if you remember that with wine, dry is the opposite of sweet. Because the sweetness level in each category can vary by producer, one brand's brut is another brand's sec.

$$$ Sparkling Wines

[yellow tail]
Pink Bubbles
AUSTRALIA

This pale, coral-colored sparkler has delicate flavors and aromas of candied citrus and strawberry. Crisp acidity balances the subtle sweetness. Light-bodied with 11.5% ABV.

Barefoot Bubbly
Brut Rosé
CALIFORNIA

More subtle and dry tasting than the label might suggest, this fizz offers sheer flavors of stone fruit (apricot), orange zest, and strawberry–rhubarb pie that taper to a nice little note of toasted piecrust. Good complexity, balance, and finesse for the price. Light-bodied with 11.5% ABV.

How Many Glasses per Bottle?

One 750ml bottle of sparkling wine yields about six 4-ounce servings. And be sure to only fill the glass half full to leave room for the all-important aromas to be captured between the wine and the rim.

BEST

**Barefoot Bubbly
Pink Moscato**
CALIFORNIA

Aromas of pink grapefruit leap out of the glass of this peachy-pink wine. Then captivating flavors of sugared ruby grapefruit immediately saturate the palate with tangy goodness—all without compromising lift and elegance. This tastes well balanced, off-dry, and refreshing, with oodles of clean, sparkling fruit flavor and a resonant finish. Light-bodied with 9.5% ABV.

$$$ Sparkling Wines

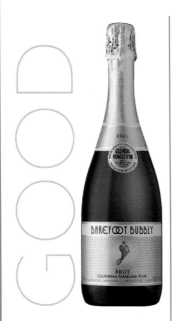

**Barefoot Bubbly
Brut**
CALIFORNIA

Alluring aromas of fresh lemon curd draw you toward that first sip. But the wine tastes a bit hollow mid-palate and vaguely like lemon meringue pie that could use a bit more flavor to take it to the next level. Light-bodied with 10.5% ABV.

**Barefoot Bubbly
Pinot Grigio**
CALIFORNIA

Expect gentle notes of sugared yellow plum and tangerine zest swirling around in this delicate sparkling wine that tastes a lot like a lighter, bubbly version of Barefoot's still style of Pinot Grigio. Good value and neither too fruity nor too subtle—just about right for that casual afternoon drink or plate of Cajun shrimp hot off the grill. Light-bodied with 11% ABV.

ROSÉ AND SPARKLING WINES

BEST

Freixenet Cordon Negro Brut Cava
SPAIN

This traditional blend of Macabeo, Xarello, and Parellado is dry, restrained, and starts with gentle aromas of green apple and salt before washing over the palate with racy, restrained flavors of sea spray, white grapefruit, and lemon zest. Lifted and well balanced. Light-bodied with 11.5% ABV.

$$$$ Sparkling Wines

Korbel
Extra Dry
CALIFORNIA

Don't mistake the words "Extra Dry" for a bone-dry wine because it's not. This bottle packs quite a lot of sweetness. Expect a mouth-filling lick of cooked apples sprinkled with brown sugar, followed by an astringent little tug on the finish. Medium-bodied with 12% ABV.

Korbel
Brut
CALIFORNIA

Quiet aromas and flavors of butter pastry and cooked apple laced with brown sugar, nutmeg, and cinnamon call to mind homemade apple crumble. The attack slowly gives way to a lingering butter and nut finish. Dry with racy acidity and impeccable balance. Quite a lot of elegance for the price. Medium-bodied with 12% ABV.

BEST

Wedding Wine

Contrary to popular belief, bone-dry bubbly doesn't work all that well with wedding cake. The tart nature of dry bubbly can taste shrill when served with sweets. The solution: Serve dry sparkling wine on its own or with savory foods, such as fish, seafood, or mushrooms Then, for a cake-time toast tipple, pour a sweeter style of bubbly—or stick with coffee.

ROSÉ AND SPARKLING WINES

Martini & Rossi
Asti
ITALY

Fresh, vivid flavors and aromas of elderflower cordial, pear, and ripe green grapes imbue this aromatic medium-sweet sparkler. Meanwhile, the high acidity ensures every sip finishes clean and dry. It's certainly an outstanding aperitif, but it's also sweet enough to pair with dessert, including wedding cake. Light-bodied with 7% ABV.

ROSÉ AND SPARKLING WINES

$$$$ Sparkling Wines

La Marca Prosecco
ITALY

With its eye-catching Tiffany-blue label and delicate, off-dry appeal, this Prosecco is an easy crowd-pleaser that teases the senses with suggestions of apricot and pear. A bit short, though, and could use a bit more concentration. Light-bodied with 11% ABV.

Cupcake Vineyards Prosecco
ITALY

Restrained in style with gentle notes of honeydew and white peach, this Prosecco is a delight. It's neither too dry nor too sweet and offers a certain creaminess that's quite fetching. Then, on the finish, a streaming note of grapefruit and Golden Delicious apple lingers. Light-bodied with 11% ABV.

Did You Know?

Classic sparkling wine corks are actually cylindrical before being compressed and inserted into bottle necks. This compression disfigures them into that familiar mushroom shape.

Korbel
Brut Rosé
CALIFORNIA

Unlike French Champagne, this Californian version blends Pinot Noir with Sangiovese, Gamay, Zinfandel, and Chenin Blanc to create a wine with flavors and aromas of red apple, honeydew, and strawberry before finishing with a soft note of pink grapefruit and nougat. Off-dry and balanced with considerable finesse. Medium-bodied with 12% ABV.

PART 5

BARGAIN WINES, DESSERT WINES, AND PARTY WINES

14

Good Deals at Super-Low Prices

Ready for a shocker? The best-selling wine in the United States comes in a box: Franzia. The second best-selling wine brand is also seriously inexpensive: Barefoot. The third in line is Carlo Rossi, which comes in those iconic jugs. In fact, five of the top 10 best-selling brands in the United States by volume cost $5 or less per 750ml—and they hail from California.

For centuries, Europeans have been making and drinking huge quantities of locally produced, inexpensive wine. Clearly, Americans are doing the same. The only difference is European jug wines tend to be drier and less fruity than their American counterparts. The disparity isn't too surprising: Europeans prefer a bit more restraint and less sugar in their wine, while Americans like a rounder, more fruit-forward style.

Although Americans drink inexpensive wine most of the time, you seldom see these wines written up or compared in newspaper columns, on blogs, or in the glossy pages of wine magazines. So how do you know which bottle or box to buy when the occasion calls for simplicity itself?

Therein lies the purpose of this chapter: to reveal the best wines at super-low prices, complete with tasting notes. All the wines recommended here cost less than $5 per 750ml.

Quite frankly, it's shocking just how many wines in this price bracket are a pleasure to drink.

$$$ Good Deals at Super-Low Prices

Charles Shaw Chardonnay
CALIFORNIA

A wine with no aroma is said to have a "closed nose," which is what we have here. Then the wine glides over the palate silky-crisp. The flavors are quite neutral, vaguely suggesting apple and citrus. Nothing glaringly wrong with this wine—it's clean and balanced—but nothing to write home about either. Medium-bodied with 12.5% ABV.

Crane Lake Chardonnay
CALIFORNIA

A bright, clean wash of Red Delicious apple and subtle pineapple flavor. Not terribly articulate but well balanced and clean, with a smooth structure and a decent amount of fruit concentration. Medium-bodied with 12.5% ABV.

**Tisdale
Chardonnay**
CALIFORNIA

The tight core of lemon curd and cooked apple flavors is laced with tangerine and toasty, nutty oak. Not only does this wine taste bright, well balanced, and texturally on point with a satiny-smooth mouthfeel, but it also offers more complexity than most Chardonnays under $5/bottle. Just lovely! Light- to medium-bodied with 12% ABV.

BARGAIN WINES, DESSERT, AND PARTY WINES

$$$ Good Deals at Super-Low Prices

Gallo Family Vineyards Chardonnay
CALIFORNIA

A butter and baked apple fragrance leads to a soft-tasting wine. In wine circles, we use the term "flabby" to describe wines that lacks acidity, which is the case here. Other than that, this gently oaked Chardonnay yields honest value with flavors of cooked apple, vanilla, and cream. To correct for the low acidity, chill it way down. Medium-bodied with 13% ABV.

Corbett Canyon Chardonnay
CALIFORNIA

From the first whiff of poached pear to the broad wash of cool, crisp orchard fruit—sliced apples and ripe pears—this wine overdelivers. It even offers a bit of complexity with grapefruit oil and warm wood threading through the lush center. A saturated, seamless, satisfying Chardonnay that tapers to a clean, dry finish. Medium-bodied with 12.5% ABV.

BEST

Glen Ellen Reserve Chardonnay
CALIFORNIA

Surprisingly concentrated, clean, and long for an under-$5 wine with unmistakable flavors and aromas of caramel apple. The texture is also invitingly mouthcoating but shot through with sufficient acidity for balance. Nice little drop to pour with pride. Medium- to full-bodied with 13.5% ABV.

$$$ Good Deals at Super-Low Prices

Livingston Cellars California Reserve Chardonnay
CALIFORNIA

Zippy and fresh with bright lemon and Granny Smith flavors swirl around in this shrill expression of Chardonnay. This wine tastes tart, slightly angular, and instantly mouthwatering. Light-bodied with 12% ABV.

Liberty Creek Chardonnay
CALIFORNIA

A promise of fresh, clean vinosity found on the nose delivers on the palate with a smooth, bright, saturated center that tastes like liquid sunshine. Granted, that flavor is difficult to parse into specific characteristics beyond mixed citrus and apple, but the texture and purity of fruit is outstanding. Well worth the money. Light- to medium-bodied with 12% ABV.

Concha y Toro Frontera Chardonnay
CHILE

Expect a bracing hit of delicious Chardonnay that tastes clean, lifted, and pure. This tightly wound wine fans out with flavors of papaya, apple, and citrus zest and a lingering grapefruit note. Impeccable balance and outstanding value for the money. Medium-bodied with 13% ABV.

$$$ Good Deals at Super-Low Prices

Franzia
Vintner Select
Chardonnay
CALIFORNIA

Aromas of baked apples lead to a tart-tasting expression with bracing flavors of Granny Smith apples laced with lemon-squirt zip. Although the razor-sharp acidity tastes a bit shrill, this wine would make an excellent spritzer by maintaining one all-important tartness factor—skip the slice of lemon! Medium-bodied with 12.5% ABV.

Peter Vella Vineyards
Chardonnay
CALIFORNIA

The aroma vaguely suggests cantaloupe; the entry is crisp and bright but not shrill; and the flavors are clean and pure, with predominately crisp apple and mixed citrus notes. This is a smooth-tasting wine with a dry finish. The flavor, though, doesn't linger at all, but this is an otherwise decent value for a wine. Light-bodied with 12% ABV.

Almaden Vineyards Heritage Chardonnay
CALIFORNIA

This is a perfectly drinkable glass of Chardonnay—clean, crisp, and well balanced. Not a lot of complexity, but the texture is smooth; the fruit is pristine, with citrus and apple flavors; and the wine offers a fair bit of concentration for the money. Medium-bodied with 13% ABV.

$$$ Good Deals at Super-Low Prices

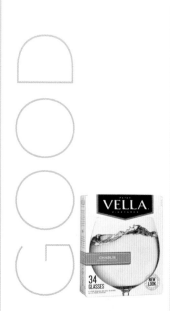

Peter Vella Vineyards Chablis
CALIFORNIA

Grapefruit aromas lead to a wash of dry white wine reminiscent of pear, sweet grapefruit, and white flowers. Smooth but short. Light-bodied with 9.5% ABV.

Livingston Cellars Chablis Blanc
CALIFORNIA

White peach aromas lead to a brisk, bright wash of vinosity. Quite neutral in terms of flavor—tasting vaguely like crisp green apple—but well balanced with a satiny mouthfeel. Good value. Light-bodied with 9.5% ABV.

BARGAIN WINES, DESSERT, AND PARTY WINES

Carlo Rossi
Chablis
CALIFORNIA

One clean, crisp sweep of unwooded Chardonnay with the classic hallmarks of bright citrus (lemon-lime), cooked apple, and even a touch of fetching salinity on the finish, which lingers. An elegant white wine for the price. Crisp and dry with the slightest whisper of sweetness to round out the edges. Light-bodied with 9.5% ABV.

$$$ Good Deals at Super-Low Prices

Gallo Family Vineyards Pinot Grigio
CALIFORNIA

This is a decent drop, but there's really not a lot going on. Bit of apple, sufficiently mouthwatering acidity, structurally correct, and balanced. Decent value. Light-bodied with 11.5% ABV.

Corbett Canyon Pinot Grigio
AUSTRALIA

This fleshy-tasting, ripe Pinot Grigio shot through with electric acidity calls to mind lemon-lime sorbet. And all that clean, juicy fruit is underpinned by an attractively chalky texture that lingers on the finish. Light-bodied with 12% ABV.

BEST

BARGAIN WINES, DESSERT, AND PARTY WINES

**Glen Ellen
Reserve
Pinot Grigio**
CALIFORNIA

With the restraint, lean structure, and lacy, lemon-scented acidity one would expect from a well-made, classic Pinot Grigio, this bottle offers excellent value for the money. True to form, the flavor profile is relatively neutral, suggesting understated fruit and wispy salinity. Light-bodied with 13% ABV.

$$$ Good Deals at Super-Low Prices

**Crane Lake
Pinot Grigio**
CALIFORNIA

Although this has the restraint and light body of a classic Pinot Grigio, it's not racy and refreshing enough to bump it up to "better" or "best" here. In short, this wine is tasty but could use a bit more mouthwatering acidity for better balance. Light-bodied with 12.5% ABV.

**Charles Shaw
Pinot Grigio**
CALIFORNIA

Light, bright, and delicious, this zingy lemon-lime-scented charmer is exactly what a decent Pinot Grigio should be. Restrained? Check. Dry and crisp? Check. Lean and clean? Check. It will have you at hello—total bargain. Light-bodied with 12.5% ABV.

Bota Box
Pinot Grigio
CALIFORNIA

Clean and steely style of Pinot Grigio with an electric shock of acidity charging the vinosity that's neutral, dry, and clean tasting. Lean, linear, and salty with a struck metal and wet stone finish. Excellent value. Light-bodied with 12% ABV.

$$$ Good Deals at Super-Low Prices

Arbor Mist
White Pear
Pinot Grigio
NEW YORK

This blend of wine and natural pear flavor is a super-sweet style that's full-throttle fruity. Expect grab-you-by-the-jugular notes of pears poached in sugar, pineapple, and lemon-lime soda. Those who like this sweeter, fruity style of beverage will enjoy it because it's well balanced and well made. Light-bodied with 6% ABV.

Carlo Rossi
California White
CALIFORNIA

Not a bad wine for the money. The aromas are gently reminiscent of apples and nougat, and the attack is bright, off-dry, and mouthwatering, with fleshy orchard fruit flavors. A bit simple but well made and balanced. Light-bodied with 10.5% ABV.

Carlo Rossi
Rhine
CALIFORNIA

Candied lime on the nose leads
to an off-dry attack of candied
lime, green apple, and ruby
grapefruit—with a sassy squeeze
of lime-squirt acidity. Easy
aperitif and outstanding value.
Light-bodied with 9% ABV.

BARGAIN WINES, DESSERT, AND PARTY WINES

Gallo Family Vineyards Sauvignon Blanc
CALIFORNIA

Fleeting aromas of grapefruit lead to a slightly dilute palate of green apples, pink grapefruit, and honeydew. Smooth, nicely toned texture. Medium-bodied with 13% ABV.

Concha y Toro Frontera Sauvignon Blanc
CHILE

Come-hither aromas of sliced red and green apple lead to a generous attack of crisp Granny Smith flavors edged with fresh basil and a fluttering of cut grass. Suave-tasting wine with gastronomic versatility. Medium-bodied with 13.5% ABV.

BEST

Gallo Family Vineyards Pink Moscato
CALIFORNIA

Exuberant aromas of honeyed peach, lychee, mixed berries, and orange lead to robust flavors of the same. The considerable sweetness is beautifully balanced with palate-cleansing acidity. This would be a great match for fresh fruit. It would also make a luscious but lively aperitif or Sunday afternoon tipple with butter pound cake. Light-bodied with 9% ABV.

$$$ Good Deals at Super-Low Prices

Richard's Wild Irish Rose Red
NEW YORK

Port-like aromas lead to a sweet hit of something that tastes a whole lot like cherry lollipops but with a big firm hit and a long orange zest finish. Full-bodied with 17% ABV.

Livingston Cellars White Zinfandel
CALIFORNIA

Gentle aromas of sugared strawberries lead to a clean, confected sweep of juicy peaches and strawberries poached in sugar. Could use a tad more lemon-squirt acidity to balance the sweetness, but otherwise, it's clean, well made, and tasty. Light-bodied with 8.5% ABV.

BEST

Gallo Family Vineyards White Zinfandel
CALIFORNIA

This great-value quaffer shines a glossy wild salmon color and brims with bright, juicy, softly sweet flavors of strawberry and white peach balanced with loads of mouthwatering freshness. A quenching wine. Light-bodied with 8.5% ABV.

$$$ Good Deals at Super-Low Prices

Arbor Mist
Exotic Fruits
White Zinfandel
NEW YORK

This wine is blended with natural flavors that the bottle says includes raspberry and lime, and it smells and tastes exactly—and I mean exactly—like grape popsicles. If you like grape popsicles, you'll love this wine. Light-bodied with 6% ABV.

Gallo Family Vineyards
Moscato
CALIFORNIA

Faint aromas of maraschino cherries lead to a lusciously sweet hit of fruit salad—with extra maraschino cherries. The ample fruit is pulled in by a seam of bright acidity. Seriously fruity and forward, this would make a budget-friendly dessert wine. Light-bodied with 9% ABV.

> **Did You Know?**
> Americans drank
> 214,889,132 liters of
> Franzia bag-in-box wine
> in 2017.

BEST

Franzia
White Zinfandel
CALIFORNIA

Shining a pretty shade of pale
pink, this popular wine exudes
faint aromas of red berries and
watermelon before slipping quite
elegantly over the palate. Silky-
soft notes of strawberry and
melon dominate this relatively
restrained rosé that finishes dry.
Light-bodied with 10.5% ABV.

$$$ Good Deals at Super-Low Prices

Crane Lake Merlot
CALIFORNIA

Dried cherries and cranberry aromas lead to a zesty, bright entry with tart cranberry notes dominating the attack and a tight little tea leaf astringency on the backtow. Medium-bodied with 12.5% ABV.

Gallo Family Vineyards Merlot
CALIFORNIA

Subtle black cherry aromas lead to approachable and refreshing black and red cherry flavors. A slight tannic texture on the finish gives it the structure to stand up to a range of foods. Full-bodied with 13% ABV.

Charles Shaw
Merlot
CALIFORNIA

Attractive aromas of black cherry and dark chocolate precede a dry, balanced entry. Ripe black forest fruits imbued with melting dark chocolate and charcoal flavors taste tightly wound, dry, and velvety. Nice length too. Good value indeed! No one would guess the price without seeing the bottle. Medium-bodied with a 12.5% ABV.

$$$ Good Deals at Super-Low Prices

Franzia
Vintner Select
Merlot
CHILE

Tart raspberry and cranberry notes taste crisp and refreshing in this bright, refreshing style of Merlot with a slightly astringent finish. Medium-bodied with 12.5% ABV.

Livingston Cellars
California Reserve
Merlot
CALIFORNIA

Vaguely berry-like aromas lead to a dilute crush of blueberries drizzled with milk chocolate, with a tug of black olive and tea on the finish. Light- to medium-bodied with 12% ABV.

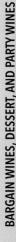

Liberty Creek
Merlot
CALIFORNIA

Warm aromas of macerated dark berries rise from the glass of this undervalued wine that tastes smooth and full of chocolate, cherry, and blackberry fruit. A nicely textured finish completes every sip. Great value. Medium-bodied with 12% ABV.

$$$ Good Deals at Super-Low Prices

Carlo Rossi
Cabernet Sauvignon
CALIFORNIA

This is a supple Cabernet
Sauvignon at a bargain price.
Expect pure black currant
aromas and flavors with a round
mouthfeel, a sweet center, and a
ripe tannic grip on the finish.
Light-bodied with 11% ABV.

Glen Ellen Reserve
Cabernet Sauvignon
CALIFORNIA

Black currant liqueur aromas are
followed by a dry, dark-fruited
entry. Not complex but nicely
concentrated and balanced with
a velvety texture. Good value
drop. Medium-bodied with
13.5% ABV.

BEST

Tisdale
Cabernet Sauvignon
CALIFORNIA

Quite a fruity, lifted expression of Cabernet Sauvignon with attractive aromas and flavors of crushed mixed red berries—especially cherries. Well made and well balanced. Definite "best" in its category. Medium-bodied with 12% ABV.

$$$ Good Deals at Super-Low Prices

Charles Shaw Cabernet Sauvignon
CALIFORNIA

Black currant nose leads to a fairly refined wine with shy notes of black currant jam, black raspberries, and a touch of black tea on the finish. Medium-bodied with 12.5% ABV.

Gallo Family Vineyards Cabernet Sauvignon
CALIFORNIA

Quiet berry scents move to a rich, robust hit of macerated black plum and mixed berries that saturate the palate. Quite pure tasting, plush, and balanced. Terrific value. Medium-bodied with 13% ABV.

Corbett Canyon
Cabernet Sauvignon
CHILE

Toasty oak underpins rather fetching flavors of black plum purée, red cherry, and cassis. This wine offers a sleek attack with a juicy center and cashmere finish. Great value. Medium-bodied with 12.5% ABV.

$$$ Good Deals at Super-Low Prices

Franzia
Vintner Select
Cabernet Sauvignon
CHILE

Aromas of poached plums and black earth lead to a ripe swirl of dark, macerated forest fruit edged with more earthy notes as well as warm wood. Robust and full with a dry black olive finish. Medium-bodied with 12.5% ABV.

Liberty Creek
Cabernet Sauvignon
CALIFORNIA

This is a clean, well-made Cabernet Sauvignon that offers honest value for the money. Sweet flavors of macerated berry fruit and raspberry coulis and hints of cassis taste ripe and robust, with the texture of crushed velvet. Good value. Medium-bodied with 12% ABV.

Almaden Vineyards Heritage Cabernet Sauvignon
CALIFORNIA

Overt aromas of raspberry jam leap from the glass and draw you toward sweet, jammy flavors of raspberry laced with Port-like notes. This is a bold style of Cabernet Sauvignon in a box. In fact, the words "deep and rich" appear on the carton, which is entirely accurate. Great value! Medium-bodied with 12.5% ABV.

$$$ Good Deals at Super-Low Prices

Gallo Family Vineyards Pinot Noir
CALIFORNIA

Coy aromas of raspberries poached in sugar lead to more of the same on the palate. This wine is juicy and sweet with a smooth mouthfeel and an abundance of stewed, succulent raspberry fruit. Medium-bodied with 12.5 ABV%.

Gallo Family Vineyards Hearty Burgundy
CALIFORNIA

Sugared plum aromas move to a smooth, fleshy entry that drenches the palate with homemade plum jam flavor. Sweet but balanced with bracing acidity. And the taste lingers with a final note of toasted almond. Medium-bodied with 12% ABV.

BEST

**Crane Lake
Pinot Noir**
CALIFORNIA

Attractively muted aromas of sun-warmed plums lead to a supple swirl of mouth-filling flavor that calls to mind cranberry sauce and a touch of earthy beetroot. Beautifully balanced with a silky mouthfeel and a textbook taste profile, this is a truly classic Pinot Noir. Excellent value. Medium-bodied with 12.5% ABV.

BARGAIN WINES, DESSERT, AND PARTY WINES

GOOD

BETTER

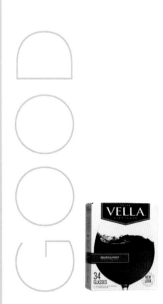

Peter Vella Vineyards Burgundy
CALIFORNIA

Vaguely reminiscent of raspberries and stewed cranberries on the nose and palate, this is a well-balanced, crisp wine. Light-bodied with 11.5% ABV.

Carlo Rossi Burgundy
CALIFORNIA

Expect a round, light, juicy wine imbued with smooth strawberry and raspberry notes. Honest value table wine. Light- to medium-bodied with 12% ABV.

Livingston Cellars Burgundy
CALIFORNIA

This light, dry, berry-scented red with an attractive note of savory earthiness subtly recalls its French namesake. Drier tasting than many other wines at this price point, this wine could be mistaken for a good quality French jug wine. Light-bodied with 11.5% ABV.

$$$ Good Deals at Super-Low Prices

GOOD

BETTER

Peter Vella Vineyards Delicious Red
CALIFORNIA

According to the box, because this is "grape wine with natural flavors," it's not just red wine. And it tastes more like cherry lollipops with an alcoholic kick than wine. If you like cherry lollipops, you'll like this wine a lot. Light-bodied with 9% ABV.

Carlo Rossi California Red
CALIFORNIA

Lovely juicy red with ample berry fruit that tastes sunlit and pure, with a dusting of cocoa powder beneath the sweet fruit center. Well balanced, well made, and pure tasting. Medium-bodied with 12% ABV.

BEST

Riunite Lambrusco
EMILIA, ITALY

A bright, bubbly hit of fresh and juicy red berry goodness makes this a quenching refresher and a hands down perfect picnic pour. Deliciousness at a great price. Light-bodied with 8% ABV.

BY APPOINTMENT TO
HM QUEEN ELIZABETH II
SHERRY SUPPLIERS
HARVEYS JEREZ, SPAIN

HARVEYS®

SINCE
1796

BRISTOL CREAM®
RICH AND FULL BODIED
SHERRY
PRODUCED AND BOTTLED BY HARVEYS IN JEREZ, SPAIN

15

Dessert Wines

Dessert wines punctuate meals perfectly, so it's quite amazing that they remain an occasional indulgence. After all, having something sweet after dinner or even lunch is pretty much a daily occurrence in the United States. I'd rather have a nip of sweet wine than a slice of chocolate cake or a big fluffy dessert any day.

This chapter rounds up all the wines in this book—from $5 to $15—that would make delicious dessert wines as well as one bottle of fortified wine: Harveys Bristol Cream.

Harveys Bristol Cream is a sweet, velvety blend of Fino, Amontillado, Oloroso, and Pedro Ximenez sherries. And don't mistake the brand to be a bit fuddy-duddy; sherry is seriously stylish these days. So decant it into a jug, pitcher, or lovely cut-crystal decanter if you have one. Any vessel will do really. Then serve it chilled with cheese and nuts or just plain pound cake—and watch guests swoon.

$$ Dessert Wines

**Barefoot
Red Moscato**
CALIFORNIA

This deep fuschia-toned rosé smells confected—much like homemade cherry pie—and ripples with lusciously sweet flavors of homemade cherry pie laced with lemon-squirt acidity. Because the bright acidity ensures perfect balance, it finishes clean and dry. Light- to medium-bodied with 9% ABV.

**Barefoot
Moscato**
CALIFORNIA

The label is right: This wine is deliciously sweet. Aromatic flavors of wildflowers, rose, dried apricot, and sun-drenched citrus oil are balanced by a bright seam of vibrant acidity—juicy and compact. Full-bodied with 9% ABV.

Woodbridge
Moscato
CALIFORNIA

Sweet marmalade and stewed apricot aromas lead to lusciously sweet flavors of mixed citrus and yellow stone fruit stewed in sugar. Because the sweetness is counterbalanced by invigorating acidity, it finishes clean and dry. Rich concentration, pristine fruit, and a polished mouthfeel combine to make this a good-value dessert wine. Light-bodied with 9.5% ABV.

$$$ Dessert Wines

**Relax
Riesling**
GERMANY

The attractive sea salt and lemon blossom perfume of this pale, straw-colored wine is followed by pronounced flavors of bright lime, juicy peach, and crisp apple. Off-dry but finishes dry. This is a sleek, accessible wine. Light-bodied with 9% ABV.

**Schmitt Söhne
Riesling**
GERMANY

A slow-to-warm-up-to-you nose of cool steel leads to a brisk, off-dry attack of green apple and lime oil edged with that cool steeliness and slight note of kerosene often found in Riesling. Taut and intense-tasting wine with a simple classicism appreciated by those who know and love German Riesling. Light-bodied with 10% ABV.

Barefoot Bubbly Pink Moscato
CALIFORNIA

Aromas of pink grapefruit leap out of the glass of this peachy-pink wine. Then captivating flavors of sugared ruby grapefruit immediately saturate the palate with tangy goodness—all without compromising lift and elegance. This tastes well balanced, off-dry, and refreshing, with oodles of clean, sparkling fruit flavor and a resonant finish. Light-bodied with 9.5% ABV.

$$$$ Dessert Wines

Roscato
Rosso Dolce (Sweet Red)
ITALY

This sweet, gently fizzy wine has soared in popularity in recent years—and it's understandable. Its succulent aromas of mixed berries shot through with a shock of balancing acidity and tiny bubbles offer an easy style of wine to pour anywhere anytime. Light-bodied with 7% ABV.

Martini & Rossi
Asti
ITALY

Fresh, vivid flavors and aromas of elderflower cordial, pear, and ripe green grapes imbue this aromatic medium-sweet sparkler. Meanwhile, the high acidity ensures every sip finishes clean and dry. It's certainly an outstanding aperitif, but it's also sweet enough to pair with dessert, including wedding cake. Light-bodied with 7% ABV.

Harveys
Bristol Cream
JEREZ DE LA FRONTERA,
SPAIN

Despite its reputation as being a bit old-fashioned, Harveys Bristol Cream is the world's best-selling Sherry—across all styles. It's amber-colored with a captivating roasted praline scent that leads to shifting flavors of toffee, toasted nut, orange oil, dates, dried currants, and sweet spices, like nutmeg, cinnamon, and clove. Full-bodied with 17.5% ABV.

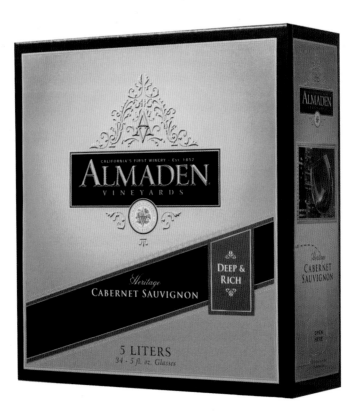

16

Party Wines

When it's party time, wine becomes so much more than a drink. It becomes a social lubricant, a point of communion, and a topic of discussion. It also displays rather conspicuously the host's personal taste, level of sophistication, and budget. No wonder the selection process can be daunting.

But pouring a simple or inexpensive wine bears no shame whatsoever; if it's undervalued, stylishly presented, and seasonally appropriate, the choice reflects better on the host or hostess than pouring something fancy, flashy, and expensive. For example, a well-made $6 White Zinfandel is the perfect pour at an outdoor wedding reception by the lake. But the same wine would look awkwardly out of place at, say, an indoor dinner party for six in December with a perfectly roasted bird or prime rib. The latter occasion calls for something distinguished and dry like a complex red or white.

That's where this chapter comes in. It presents the good, better, and best wines for every type of party, taking into account mood, setting, and decorum. Every wine recommended here has broad general appeal, is unquestionably appropriate, and is arguably undervalued. So without further ado …

Party Wines
WEDDING RECEPTION

WHITES

Ruffino Orvieto Classic, Italy
($$)
(see p. 80)

GOOD

Cavit Collection Pinot Grigio, Italy
($$$)
(see p. 64)

BETTER

Placido Pinot Grigio, Italy
($$)
(see p. 59)

BEST

REDS

Lindeman's Bin 45 Cabernet Sauvignon, Australia
($$)
(see p. 102)

GOOD

Beringer Founders' Estate Cabernet Sauvignon, California
($$$)
(see p. 109)

BETTER

Columbia Crest Grand Estates Cabernet Sauvignon, Washington
($$$)
(see p. 111)

BEST

Wine Selection Criteria

Wedding reception reds and whites should have a classic air about them. They should be agreeable enough to appeal to all guests without tasting dull or boring. And they should pair easily with food, be widely available, and have reasonable prices. Tick all these boxes and you're on track.

Party Wines
WEDDING RECEPTION

ROSÉS

Sutter Home White Zinfandel, California ($$) (see p. 156)

Barefoot White Zinfandel, California ($$) (see p. 156)

Beringer White Zinfandel, California ($$) (see p. 157)

SPARKLING

La Marca Prosecco, Italy ($$$$) (see p. 170)

Korbel Brut California Champagne, California ($$$$) (see p. 168)

Korbel Brut Rosé California Champagne, California ($$$$) (see p. 171)

How Much Wine Do You Need?

Estimate that each guest will have two glasses in the first hour and one glass for every hour after that. Multiply that number by the number of guests to determine how many glasses you need. Each 750mL bottle contains five 150mL servings; divide the total number of glasses by five to determine the number of bottles you'll need.

Party Wines
WEDDING RECEPTION

DESSERT

Schmitt Söhne Riesling, Germany ($$$)
(see p. 218)

GOOD

Woodbridge Moscato, California ($$)
(see p. 217)

BETTER

Martini & Rossi Asti, Italy ($$$$)
(see p. 220)

BEST

Party Wines
DINNER PARTY

WHITES

Kendall-Jackson Vintner's Reserve Chardonnay, California ($$$$)
(see p. 52)

Chateau St. Jean Chardonnay, California ($$$$)
(see p. 49)

Wente Morning Fog Chardonnay, California ($$$$)
(see p. 55)

REDS

Beringer Founders' Estate Cabernet Sauvignon, California ($$$)
(see p. 109)

Columbia Crest Grand Estates Cabernet Sauvignon, Washington ($$$)
(see p. 111)

Josh Cellars Legacy Red Wine, California ($$$)
(see p. 95)

Wine Selection Criteria

Dinner party wines should be complex, elegant, refined bottles that enhance the food but not overpower it. Labels should also be attractive because the bottles will grace tables. And if a wine isn't particularly well suited to an occasion, decant it into a pretty jug. Lastly, selecting a wine by a reputable producer suggests you know your stuff—and you should with this book's help.

Party Wines
DINNER PARTY

SPARKLING

La Marca
Prosecco,
Italy
($$$)
(see p. 170)

Korbel Brut
California
Champagne,
California
($$$$)
(see p. 168)

Korbel Brut
Rosé California
Champagne,
California
($$$)
(see p. 171)

DESSERT

Schmitt Söhne
Riesling,
Germany
($$$)
(see p. 218)

Woodbridge
Moscato,
California
($$)
(see p. 81)

Harveys
Bristol Cream,
Spain
($$$$)
(see p. 221)

Etiquette Tip

Must the host or hostess open the bottle of wine a guest brings to a dinner party? Absolutely not. And yes, it's usually rude for the guest to suggest it.

Party Wines

WHITES

Ruffino Orvieto Classico, Italy
($$)
(see p. 80)

Cavit Collection Pinot Grigio, Italy
($$$)
(see p. 64)

Placido Pinot Grigio, Italy
($$)
(see p. 59)

REDS

Lindeman's Bin 45 Cabernet Sauvignon, Australia
($$)
(see p. 102)

Beringer Founders' Estate Cabernet Sauvignon, California
($$$)
(see p. 109)

Columbia Crest Grand Estates Cabernet Sauvignon, Washington
($$$)
(see p. 111)

GOOD

BETTER

BEST

BARGAIN WINES, DESSERT WINES, AND PARTY WINES

Party Wines
COCKTAIL PARTY

ROSÉS

GOOD

Sutter Home
White Zinfandel,
California
($$)
(see p. 156)

BETTER

Barefoot
White Zinfandel,
California
($$)
(see p. 156)

BEST

Beringer
White
Zinfandel,
California
($$)
(see p. 157)

SPARKLING

GOOD

La Marca
Prosecco,
Italy
($$$)
(see p. 170)

BETTER

Korbel Brut
California
Champagne,
California
($$$$)
(see p. 168)

BEST

Korbel Brut
Rosé California
Champagne,
California
($$$)
(see p. 171)

Party Wines
BACKYARD BARBECUE

WHITES

GOOD

Tisdale
Chardonnay,
California
($$$)
(see p. 177)

BETTER

Glen Ellen
Reserve
Chardonnay,
California
($$$)
(see p. 179)

BEST

Bota Box
Pinot Grigio,
California
($$$)
(see p. 189)

REDS

GOOD

Charles Shaw
Merlot,
California
($$$)
(see p. 199)

BETTER

Corbett Canyon
Cabernet
Sauvignon,
Chile
($$$)
(see p. 205)

BEST

Almaden
Vineyards
Heritage
Cabernet
Sauvignon,
California
($$$)
(see p. 207)

Wine Selection Criteria

Backyard barbecues require full-fruited wines that stand up
to the charred flavors of grilled foods. And because
barbecues are typically held in warm weather, the wines need
a good balance of acidity to keep guests feeling refreshed
after each sip.

Party Wines
BACKYARD BARBECUE

ROSÉS

GOOD

**Gallo Family
Vineyards
White Zinfandel,
California
($$$)**
(see p. 195)

BETTER

**Beringer
White Zinfandel,
California
($$)**
(see p. 157)

BEST

**Franzia
White
Zinfandel,
California
($$$)**
(see p. 197)

WHITES

REDS

GOOD

**Peter Vella
Vineyards,
Chardonnay,
California
($$$)**
(see p. 182)

GOOD

**Corbett Canyon
Cabernet
Sauvignon,
Chile
($$$)**
(see p. 205)

BETTER

**Carlo Rossi
Chablis,
California
($$$)**
(see p. 185)

BETTER

**Almaden
Vineyards
Heritage
Cabernet
Sauvignon,
California
($$$)**
(see p. 207)

BEST

**Almaden
Vineyards
Heritage
Chardonnay,
California
($$$)**
(see p. 183)

BEST

**Crane Lake
Pinot Noir,
California
($$$)**
(see p. 209)

Wine Selection Criteria

For those quintessentially casual affairs, feel free to venture into the world of alternative packaging, such as boxes; always include some light and quenching choices; and let the good times roll.

Party Wines
BEACH/POOL/COTTAGE PARTY

ROSÉS

GOOD

**Gallo Family
Vineyards
White Zinfandel,
California
($$$)**
(see p. 195)

BETTER

**Beringer
White Zinfandel,
California
($$)**
(see p. 157)

BEST

**Franzia
White
Zinfandel,
California
($$$)**
(see p. 197)

Party Wines
GARDEN PARTY

WHITES

REDS

GOOD

Ruffino
Orvieto Classico,
Italy
($$)
(see p. 80)

GOOD

Folonari
Pinot Noir,
Italy
($$)
(see p. 133)

BETTER

Cavit Collection
Pinot Grigio,
Italy
($$$)
(see p. 64)

BETTER

J. Lohr Los Osos
Merlot,
California
($$$$)
(see p. 129)

BEST

Placido
Pinot Grigio,
Italy
($$)
(see p. 59)

BEST

Estancia
Vineyards
Pinot Noir,
California
($$$$)
(see p. 137)

Wine Selection Criteria

Garden parties hail from Britain and have a whiff of frilly formality to them. Therefore, the wines should be crisp, refreshing, and of a high standard. And never forget a chilled Moscato with peaches and cream for dessert! Or maybe a good old-fashioned Harveys Bristol Cream—on the rocks.

BARGAIN WINES, DESSERT WINES, AND PARTY WINES

235

Party Wines
GARDEN PARTY

ROSÉS

GOOD

Sutter Home White Zinfandel, California ($$)
(see p. 156)

BETTER

Barefoot White Zinfandel, California ($$)
(see p. 156)

BEST

Beringer White Zinfandel, California ($$)
(see p. 157)

SPARKLING

GOOD

La Marca Prosecco, Italy ($$$)
(see p. 170)

BETTER

Korbel Brut California Champagne, California ($$$$)
(see p. 168)

BEST

Korbel Brut Rosé California Champagne, California ($$$)
(see p. 171)

DESSERT

GOOD

**Schmitt Söhne
Riesling,
Germany
($$$)**
(see p. 218)

BETTER

**Woodbridge
Moscato,
California
($$)**
(see p. 217)

BEST

**Harveys
Bristol Cream,
Spain
($$$$)**
(see p. 221)

BARGAIN WINES, DESSERT WINES, AND PARTY WINES

Party Wines
BANQUET

WHITES

Ruffino Orvieto Classico, Italy ($$)
(see p. 80)

Cavit Collection Pinot Grigio, Italy ($$$)
(see p. 64)

Placido Pinot Grigio, Italy ($$)
(see p. 59)

REDS

Lindeman's Bin 45 Cabernet Sauvignon, Australia ($$)
(see p. 102)

Jacob's Creek Classic Cabernet Sauvignon, Australia ($$)
(see p. 107)

Beringer Founders' Estate Cabernet Sauvignon, California ($$$)
(see p. 109)

Wine Selection Criteria

Banquets call for food-friendly choices that are classic and inexpensive but not deadly dull or dirt cheap. And all that's required is a red and a white.

PART **6**

APPENDIX

Hidden Gems

As a wine writer, I regularly come across bottles that should be bestsellers but aren't. In this chapter, I reveal several of my current favorites that fit that description and are well worth tasting. These are under-$15 bottles that deliver excellent value for the money, show minimal vintage variation, and might not be as widely available as the other wines in this book—but have decent distribution and are worth scouting out. If you see them on shelves, snap them up. And if you don't, ask your favorite wine merchant to stock them. Or go to www.wine-searcher.com to see where they're stocked near you.

Straying from the format of the rest of this book, I've grouped them all together because they're all "bests."

Here's to the thrill of finding truly delicious undervalued juice.

Hidden Gems

Quinta da Aveleda
Vinho Verde
($$$)
PORTUGAL

Scents of bay leaf and lime blossom rise from the glass and draw you in before the tense, cool, tightly wound beam of flavor glides in all saturated and pure and unravels with green apple, grapefruit, lime oil, salt, and bay leaf notes that resonate on the finish. So articulate, smooth, and racy. Light-bodied with 11% ABV.

Segura Viudas
Brut Cava
($$$)
CATALONIA, SPAIN

Subdued scents of orange and grapefruit zest, toast, and lilac lead to an electric, mouthwatering attack of salted grapefruit edged with lime and freshly baked bread. The aromas, flavors, and structure of this dry Cava come together in an impressive whole that doesn't vary much from year to year. Light-bodied with 12% ABV.

Piera Martellozzo Blu Giovello Prosecco ($$$)
VENETO, ITALY

Here, find Prosecco's characteristic note of pear imbued with bitter orange and white grapefruit that yields a compelling finish and seasons the palate beautifully. The hint of sweetness is balanced with lemon-squirt acidity, so it finishes clean and dry. Light-bodied with 11% ABV.

Bollini Pinot Grigio ($$$$)
TRENTINO, ITALY

This starts with a gentle perfume of subdued citrus and chalk before slipping across the palate with saturated but understated stone fruit and lemon laced with chalk, salt, and white grapefruit edged with smoke and flint. A lot of complexity for a Pinot Grigio without straying from the style's restrained classicism. Light- to medium-bodied with 13% ABV.

Hidden Gems

Villa Maria Sauvignon Blanc ($$$$)
MARLBOROUGH, NEW ZEALAND

This wine's full-throttle flavor is immediately captivating. The attack of juicy guava fruit is dappled with orange, lemon, and lime and underpinned with notes of coriander, parsley, and grapefruit zest, creating an intriguingly complex experience. Clean, satiny, and versatile. Light-bodied with 12.5% ABV.

The Ned Sauvignon Blanc ($$$$)
MARLBOROUGH, NEW ZEALAND

While some crisp whites scream summer, the weight and power of this zesty New Zealand Sauvignon Blanc keep it relevant for all seasons. So if you're a fan of the style, try this incredible value thriller. Dry and crisp with full-throttle flavors of damp herbs, cucumber, and lime. Medium-bodied with 13% ABV.

Michael David Winery The Seven Deadly Zins Zinfandel
($$$$)
LODI, CALIFORNIA

Rich, powerful, and spicy, this Zinfandel blended with Petite Sirah and Petit Verdot explodes with muscular cherry and blackberry fruit layered with pepper and black earth. A seriously lush, hedonistic, and long red wine. Full-bodied with 14.5% ABV.

Wolf Blass Yellow Label Cabernet Sauvignon
($$$$)
AUSTRALIA

This expression of Cabernet Sauvignon saturates the palate with dry, harmonious flavors of black plum, black cherry, cassis, coffee, cocoa powder, toasted nut, and vanilla bean that linger. Oak maturation contributes a whisper of wood that adds texture and complexity—but it's well integrated. Full-bodied with 13.5% ABV.

Index

A

Alamos
  Cabernet Sauvignon, 120
  Chardonnay, 50
  Malbec, 147
  Red Blend, 94
  Torrontés, 85
alcohol level, Chardonnay, 35
Almaden Vineyards
  Heritage Cabernet Sauvignon,
    207, 231, 233
  Heritage Chardonnay, 183,
    233
André sparkling wine
  Brut, 162
  Brut Rosé, 163
Apothic
  Red, 92
  White, 84
Arbor Mist
  Exotic Fruits White Zinfandel,
    196
  White Pear Pinot Grigio, 190

B

backyard barbecue wines, 233–234
bag-in-box wines, 16–17
Banfi Centine red blend, 92
banquet wines, 241
Barefoot
  Bubbly Brut, 166
  Bubbly Brut Rosé, 164
  Bubbly Pink Moscato, 165,
    219
  Bubbly Pinot Grigio, 166
  Cabernet Sauvignon, 104
  Chardonnay, 38
  Merlot, 125
  Moscato, 80, 216
  Pink Moscato, 154

  Pinot Grigio, 63
  Red Moscato, 154, 216
  Rosé, 155
  Sauvignon Blanc, 73
  White Zinfandel, 156, 225,
    230, 236
  Zinfandel, 140
beach/pool/cottage party wines,
  235–36
Bella Sera Pinot Grigio, 58
Beringer
  Founders' Estate Cabernet
    Sauvignon, 109, 224, 227,
    229, 238
  Founders' Estate Chardonnay,
    41
  Main & Vine Cabernet
    Sauvignon, 106
  Main & Vine Chardonnay, 34
  White Zinfandel, 157, 225,
    230, 232, 234, 236
Black Box
  Cabernet Sauvignon, 101
  Pinot Grigio, 60
Blackstone Cabernet Sauvignon
  Cabernet Sauvignon, 108
Bogle Vineyards
  Chardonnay, 43
  Essential Red, 97
  Merlot, 126
  Petite Sirah, 146
Bollini Pinot Grigio, 245
Bonterra Chardonnay, 48
Bota Box Pinot Grigio, 189, 231
Burgundy's Chardonnay, 47

C

Cabernet Sauvignon, 99–121
  biggest markets, 113
  food pairing tip, 103
  myth, 109

Canyon Road
    Cabernet Sauvignon, 100
    Chardonnay, 36
Carlo Rossi
    Burgundy, 210
    Cabernet Sauvignon, 202
    California Red, 212
    California White, 190
    Chablis, 185, 235
    Rhine, 191
Carmenere, 145
Carnivor
    Cabernet Sauvignon, 116
    Zinfandel, 148
Cavit Collection Pinot Grigio, 64,
    224, 229, 235, 238
Chardonnay, 31–55
    alcohol level, 35
    calories, 37
    food pairing tip, 33, 41, 51
    ideal serving temperature, 33
Charles Shaw
    Cabernet Sauvignon, 204
    Chardonnay, 176
    Merlot, 199, 231
    Pinot Grigio, 188
Chateau Souverain
    Cabernet Sauvignon, 116
    Chardonnay, 52
Chateau Ste. Michelle Chardonnay,
    54
Chateau St. Jean
    Cabernet Sauvignon, 114
    Chardonnay, 49, 227
Chianti, 91
cocktail party wines, 230–232
color, 21
Columbia Crest
    Grand Estates Cabernet
        Sauvignon, 111, 224, 227,
        229

Grand Estates Chardonnay,
    47
Grand Estates Merlot, 127
H3 Cabernet Sauvignon, 121
Columbia Winery
    Cabernet Sauvignon, 118
    Chardonnay, 51
Concannon Petite Sirah, 149
Concha y Toro
    Casillero del Diablo
        Carmenere, 144
    Casillero del Diablo Reserva
        Cabernet Sauvignon, 108
    Casillero del Diablo
        Sauvignon Blanc, 75
    Frontera Cabernet Sauvignon,
        100
    Frontera Chardonnay, 181
    Frontera Sauvignon Blanc, 192
Cook's Brut sparkling wine, 162
Corbett Canyon
    Cabernet Sauvignon, 205,
        231, 233
    Chardonnay, 178
    Pinot Grigio, 186
Crane Lake
    Chardonnay, 176
    Merlot, 198
    Pinot Grigio, 188
    Pinot Noir, 209, 233
Cupcake Vineyards
    Chardonnay, 40
    Prosecco, 170
    Red Velvet, 93
    Sauvignon Blanc, 74

D

Dark Horse
    The Original Cabernet
        Sauvignon, 110

The Original Chardonnay, 46
The Original Pinot Grigio, 65
dessert wine, 215–21
dinner party wines, 227–228

E

Ecco Domani Pinot Grigio, 69
Edna Valley Vineyard Chardonnay,
    53
Estancia Vineyards
    Cabernet Sauvignon, 119
    Chardonnay, 48
    Pinot Grigio, 68
    Pinot Noir, 137, 235

F

Fetzer
    Eagle Peak Merlot, 126
    Gewürztraminer, 83
    Sundial Chardonnay, 44
    Valley Oaks Cabernet
        Sauvignon, 112
Fish Eye
    Chardonnay, 35
    Pinot Grigio, 62
flawed bottle, 14
Flipflop
    Cabernet Sauvignon, 103
    Chardonnay, 33
    Pinot Grigio, 60
Folonari
    Chianti, 91
    Pinot Grigio, 61
    Pinot Noir, 133, 235
food pairing tips
    Cabernet Sauvignon, 103
    Chardonnay, 33, 41, 51
    Merlot, 127
    other great reds, 141
    Pinot Noir, 133

red blends, 91, 93
Riesling, 83
Ruffino Orvieto Classico, 81
Sauvignon Blanc, 75, 77
sparkling wine, 167
14 Hands Winery
    Cabernet Sauvignon, 117
    Hot to Trot Red Blend, 94
    Merlot, 128
Franzia
    Merlot, 200
    Vintner Select Cabernet
        Sauvignon, 206
    Vintner Select Chardonnay,
        182
    White Zinfandel, 197, 232,
        234
Freixenet Cordon Negro Brut Cava
    sparkling wine, 167

G

Gallo Family Vineyards
    Cabernet Sauvignon, 204
    Chardonnay, 178
    Hearty Burgundy, 208
    Merlot, 198
    Moscato, 196
    Pink Moscato, 193
    Pinot Grigio, 186
    Pinot Noir, 208
    Sauvignon Blanc, 192
    White Zinfandel, 195, 232,
        234
garden party wines, 237–240
Glen Ellen Reserve
    Cabernet Sauvignon, 202
    Chardonnay, 179, 231
    Pinot Grigio, 187
Gnarly Head
    Chardonnay, 40

Old Vine Zinfandel, 145
Pinot Noir, 135
good deals, 175–213
grapes
Cabernet Sauvignon, 111
grown at higher altitudes, 121
organically grown, 49
Pinot Grigio, 59

H–I

Harveys Bristol Cream, 221, 228, 235, 237
hidden gems, 245–249
historic winery, 55

J

Jacob's Creek
Classic Cabernet Sauvignon, 107, 238
Classic Chardonnay, 36
Classic Shiraz, 143
Classic Shiraz Cabernet, 90
J. Lohr
Los Osos Merlot, 129, 235
Syrah, 146
Joel Gott Sauvignon Blanc, 76
Josh Cellars
Chardonnay, 50
Legacy Red Wine, 95, 227
Rosé, 158
Sauvignon Blanc, 76

K

Kendall-Jackson Vintner's Reserve
Chardonnay, 52, 227
Kim Crawford Rosé, 158
Korbel
Brut California Champagne, 168, 225, 228, 230, 236

Brut Rosé California
Champagne, 171, 225, 228, 230, 236
Extra Dry sparkling wine, 168
kosher wine, 143

L

La Marca Prosecco, 170, 225, 228, 230, 236
leftover wine, preserving of, 20
Liberty Creek
Cabernet Sauvignon, 206
Chardonnay, 180
Merlot, 201
Lindeman's
Bin 45 Cabernet Sauvignon, 102, 224, 229, 235, 238
Bin 65 Chardonnay, 32
Bin 85 Pinot Grigio, 58
Bin 50 Shiraz, 141
Livingston Cellars
Burgundy, 211
California Reserve
Chardonnay, 180
California Reserve Merlot, 200
Chablis Blanc, 184
White Zinfandel, 194
low-priced wine. See 175–213
luxury wine, 15

M

Malbec, 147
Manischewitz
Blackberry, 142
Concord Grape, 142
Mark West Pinot Noir, 134
Martini & Rossi Asti, 169, 220, 226
M. Chapoutier Les Vignes de
Bila-Haut, 84

Good, Better, Best Wines, Second Edition

Ménage à Trois
  California Red Wine, 96
  Silk Soft Red Blend, 96
Merlot, 123-29
  brownie recipe, 125
  food pairing tip, 127
  history, 129
  "Sideways Effect," 123
  standard pour, 129
Mezzacorona
  Cliffhanger Vineyards Pinot
    Grigio, 68
  Estate Bottled Cabernet
    Sauvignon, 106
  Estate Bottled Chardonnay, 39
  Estate Bottled Pinot Grigio, 66
  Estate Bottled Pinot Noir, 132
Michael David Winery: The Seven
  Deadly Zins Zinfandel, 247
Mirassou Winery Pinot Noir, 134
Moscato, 81

N

The Ned Sauvignon Blanc, 246
19 Crimes Cabernet Sauvignon,
  113
Nobilo Sauvignon Blanc, 74
Noble Vines
  Collection 337 Cabernet
    Sauvignon, 118
  Collection Chardonnay, 44
  Collection 667 Pinot Noir,
    136

O

organically grown grapes, 49
other great reds, 139-49
  food pairing tip, 141
  history, 141
other great whites, 79-85

  food pairing tip, 81
Oyster Bay
  Chardonnay, 54
  Pinot Noir, 136
  Sauvignon Blanc, 77

P–Q

packaging, 16
palate, 24
party wines, 223-241
  backyard barbecue,
    233-234
  banquet, 241
  beach/pool/cottage party,
    235-36
  cocktail party, 230-232
  dinner party, 227-228
  etiquette tip, 228
  garden party, 237-240
  wedding reception, 224-226
Peter Vella Vineyards
  Burgundy, 210
  Chablis, 184
  Chardonnay, 182, 2353
  Delicious Red, 212
Petite Sirah, 147
Piera Martellozzo Blu Giovello
  Prosecco, 245
Pinot Grigio, 57-69
Pinot Noir, 131-137
  challenge of making, 137
  food pairing tip, 133
  history, 135
Placido Pinot Grigio, 59, 224, 229,
  235, 238
popular wine, 15
premium wine, 15
price, 15

Quinta da Aveleda Vinho Verde,
  244

Index

R

red blends, 89–97
    food pairing tip, 91, 93
Relax Riesling, 82, 218
Rex Goliath: The Giant 47 Pound
  Rooster
    Cabernet Sauvignon, 105
    Pinot Grigio, 62
Richard's Wild Irish Rose Red, 194
Riesling, 83
Riunite Lambrusco, 213
Robert Mondavi Private Selection
  Merlot, 128
Roscato
    Rosé Dolce (Sweet Rosé),
      159
    Rosso Dolce (Sweet Red),
      148, 220
rosé, 153–59
    sweetness and body, 155
Ruffino
    Chianti, 90
    Lumina Pinot Grigio, 67
    Orvieto Classico, 80, 224, 229,
      235, 238

S

Santa Rita
    Reserva Cabernet Sauvignon,
      114
    120 Reserva Especial
      Cabernet Sauvignon, 110
Sauvignon Blanc, 71–77
    food pairing tip, 75, 77
Schmitt Söhne Riesling, 82, 218,
  226, 228, 237
screw caps, 14
Segura Viudas Brut Cava, 244
serving, 21–24
    color, 21

drinking order, 24
food, 23–24
glasses, 22–23
palate, 24
temperature, 21–22, 33, 61
"universal" glass, 23
Shiraz, 141
"Sideways Effect," 123, 131, 133
Smoking Loon
    The Original Cabernet
      Sauvignon, 112
    The Original Chardonnay, 42
    The Original Old Vine
      Zinfandel, 144
    The Original Pinot Grigio, 66
    Steelbird Chardonnay, 46
sparkling wine, 161–71
    corks, 171
    food pairing tip, 167
    servings per bottle, 165
    sweetness, 163
    wedding wine, 169
Stemmari
    Pinot Grigio, 64
    Pinot Noir, 132
stemware, 22
Sterling Vineyards
    Chardonnay, 42
    Vintner's Collection Cabernet
      Sauvignon, 120
storage, 19–21
    bright light, 19–20
    dramatic temperature
      fluctuation, 21
    exposure to oxygen, 20
    heat, 21
    leftover wine, preserving of,
      20
    light-struck aromas, 20
super luxury wine, 15
super premium wine, 15

Sutter Home
    Family Vineyards Chardonnay,
        34
    White Zinfandel, 156, 225,
        230, 236
Sycamore Lane
    Cabernet Sauvignon, 102
    Chardonnay, 37
Syrah, 141

T

tannins, 20
tasting, 25–26
temperature, 21–22
Tisdale
    Cabernet Sauvignon, 203
    Chardonnay, 177, 231
Toasted Head
    Barrel Aged Cabernet
        Sauvignon, 115
    Barrel Aged Chardonnay, 45
Torrontés, 85
trade secrets, 13–17
    bag-in-box wines, 16–17
    flawed bottle, 14
    luxury wine, 15
    packaging, 16
    popular wine, 15
    premium wine, 15
    price, 15
    screw caps, 14
    super luxury wine, 15
    super premium wine, 15
    ultra premium wine, 15
    value wine, 15
    vintage and aging, 15–16

U–V

ultra premium wine, 15
"universal" glass, 23

value wine, 15
Villa Maria Sauvignon Blanc, 246
vintage and aging, 15–16

W–X

wedding reception wines, 169,
    224–226
Wente Morning Fog Chardonnay,
    55, 227
White Zinfandel, 157
winery
    historic, 55
    zero-waste, 45
Wolf Blass Yellow Label Cabernet
    Sauvignon, 247
Woodbridge by Robert Mondavi
    Chardonnay, 32
    Merlot, 124
    Moscato, 81, 217, 226, 228,
        237
    Sauvignon Blanc, 72

Y–Z

[yellow tail]
    Cabernet Sauvignon, 104
    Chardonnay, 38
    Merlot, 124
    Pink Bubbles sparkling wine,
        163
    Sauvignon Blanc, 72
    Shiraz, 140

Zalto wine glass, 23
zero-waste winery, 45
Zinfandel, 149

About the Author

Carolyn Evans Hammond is an internationally recognized writer and media personality who fell in love with wine during her first trip to France many moons ago when she picnicked in the vineyards of the Côtes du Rhône. Now she makes wine accessible with her witty and light approach to the topic.

Photograph by Tim Leyes
Hair and makeup by Jessica Haisinger

Carolyn is a two-time bestselling wine book author, the wine columnist for the *Toronto Star*, and a seasoned wine judge. She believes living well doesn't have to be pricey or pretentious. It just takes a little know-how—and maybe a corkscrew.

Her first book, *1000 Best Wine Secrets*, is a fascinating compilation of trade secrets designed to illuminate the topic and help wine drinkers make more satisfying wine choices. It earned critical acclaim and international distribution.

Her second book, *Good Better Best Wines: A No-Nonsense Guide to Popular Wines*, ranks the best-selling wines in the United States up to $15. It was an instant success, and this book is an updated version of that title.

Over the past 15 years, she has appeared on CNN International, BON TV (China), GoingGlobalTV.com, Canada AM, and CITY-TV; she has been a guest on radio stations all over the United States; and she has written for top publications, including *Decanter*, *Wine Spectator*, *Wine & Spirit International*, *The Times* (London), *Maclean's*, *Quench*, *Taste*, and others.

Carolyn's a longstanding member of the Circle of Wine Writers, holds a diploma from the Wine & Spirit Education Trust in the UK, and earned a BA from York University, where she studied English and philosophy. She has lived in many cities in North America and Europe and now resides in Toronto, where she was born.

Contact Carolyn via social media or email:
Twitter: *@thewinefind*
Instagram: *carolynevanshammond*
Email: *carolyn@carolynevanshammond.com*

Acknowledgments

Thanks to all the people who have gone out of their way to provide the samples, images, and information needed to make this book happen. Thanks also to my agent Jessica Faust and editor Christopher Stolle.

Publisher Mike Sanders
Editor Christopher Stolle
Book Designer William Thomas
Compositor Ayanna Lacey
Proofreader Jana M. Stefanciosa
Indexer Celia McCoy

First American Edition, 2018
Published in the United States by DK Publishing
6081 E. 82nd Street, Indianapolis, Indiana 46250

Copyright © 2018 Dorling Kindersley Limited
DK, a Division of Penguin Random House LLC
18 19 20 21 22   10 9 8 7 6 5 4 3 2 1

001–311015–NOVEMBER/2018

ISBN 978-1-4654-7666-1
Library of Congress Catalog Number: 2018935997

DK books are available at special discounts when purchased in bulk for sales
promotions, premiums, fund-raising, or educational use. For details, contact:
DK Publishing Special Markets, 345 Hudson Street, New York, New York
10014
SpecialSales@dk.com

Printed and bound in China
All images © Dorling Kindersley Limited
For further information see: www.dkimages.com

A WORLD OF IDEAS:
SEE ALL THERE IS TO KNOW

www.dk.com